Here, And Always Have Been

An Anthology of Gay Historical Fiction

First Edition

Published by The Nazca Plains Corporation
Las Vegas, Nevada
2009

ISBN: 978-1-935509-43-1

Published by

The Nazca Plains Corporation ®
4640 Paradise Rd, Suite 141
Las Vegas NV 89109-8000

PUBLISHER'S NOTE
Here, And Always Have Been is a work of fiction created wholly by *Kenneth Craigside's* imagination. All characters are fictional and any resemblance to any persons living or deceased is purely by accident. No portion of this book reflects any real person or events.

Cover Photo, Patrick Hermans
Art Director, Blake Stephens

Dedication

In loving memory of David Trimble and Frank Dunand.

Here, And Always Have Been

An Anthology of Gay Historical Fiction

First Edition

Kenneth Craigside

Contents

Stalagmite

Out there it was bitter cold and dangerous. This was the day foretold by the elders—the shortest day—the day that the people most feared as they huddled around their fires, and the day that all of the animals snuggled further into dens and burrows. A day so cold that the spirits fled to the deepest fissures of the Earth, and even the strongest spirit of all, the Sun, fought to rise into the icy sky, and then too soon after sank, exhausted, beyond the edge of the world. This was the time when the spirits must be somehow calmed and implored to return. The animals as well. And it would also be the night of the ceremony when boys received their man-spirits.

In here it was safe and warm. The fire made it even warmer. Deep in Earth's sacred womb, two men prepared for the ceremony. It was so warm that the two had shed their fur cloaks and leggings. Sweat made their naked bodies shine in the firelight. The youngest, who had known seventeen such shortest days, held a torch up to the undulating limestone wall. The other, who had survived thirty winters, picked up a small hollow tube made from a bird's bone. He dipped one end of it into a gourd filled with powdered ash, and then, by blowing through the other end, dusted black shadows of roundness on the still-wet painting of a leaping stag.

"Hold the torch closer."

"Why did the elders want you to make stags this time?"

"You know why."

"I have not seen many stags."

"That is why."

"To cause them to come."

"Yes."

"Last winter, when you made the bison, not many came."

"Then I did not make them well enough."

"But these will force the stags to come."

"You think so? Why?"

"You make them leaping and happy."

"And those bison?"

"Just stood and ate grass."

"Ah."

The painter put down his bird bone and picked up a kind of reed. Its end had been beaten and scraped into little hairs so that it would hold the color. Then he reached for another gourd in which the black ash powder had been mixed with bear grease.

"Now hold the torch higher."

"Antlers?"

"Yes."

The older man studied the painted stag for a moment. Next he reached up to feel the curve of the wall. Then with fast smooth movements and sudden swooping flips, he dashed in the antlers.

"That is magic that they cannot resist," said the younger.

"We will see. Take your torch over here."

Another stag, and again the sure swoops of his brush.

"Such magic. How did you learn it?"

"By looking."

"I look, but I could not do that."

"Maybe not enough."

"I hunt. I look."

Now a third one had its antlers.

"You look for where the animal will run and where your spear will go."

"Yes."

"But do not stop to see the whole spirit of the animal."

"Maybe."

Three fully antlered stags, near life-size, now leaped across the cavern wall. The two men retired to their fire. All around were paintings of animals. They covered the walls and even spread up onto the ceiling. Some had been painted over with others. And here and there, as high as a boy or man could reach were outlines of human hands. Outlines that had been made for each new-man's hand at the end of the ceremony, by blowing the black ash over as the once-boy reached up and held his palm to the wall. There were hundreds of them, for the cave was sacred and had been reserved for this purpose forever.

"Which is yours?' asked the older man.

"My what?"

"Hand mark."

The younger walked over to the painting of a mammoth, and placed his hand over one of the prints.

"This one."

"You're taller now."

"Yes."

"Look at your hand, then look at its mark."

"Yes?"

"Keep looking. Read the pattern in each. See the spirit of your hand. Now take this reed and the gourd of black, and make the magic of a hand."

The younger found a lower blank space and started to trace his hand.

"No. Do not do not take the reed around it. Hold your hand away, look at it, and make its spirit on the stone."

He looked and tried, but the reed made wavy lines more like some strange leaf than a hand.

"If you looked many more times, and reeded even more, you could do it."

"Is that how you learned?"

"No, an elder taught me, one who's spirit has been taken. But somehow I knew."

"How could that be?"

"I knew how to look, even as a little boy I knew this."

"But boys do not hunt."

"No, but they can still look. And then, when they look enough they can see like- spirits."

"Like-spirits?"

"Things that look the same, as when a dark cloud rumbles up and takes the shape of a mammoth, or when dogs run and jump like leaping elks, or a rounded rock seems to be a sleeping bear. Those are like-spirits. When you can see the patterns in things, then you can make the picture magic."

"No, there must be more than that. I can see like-spirits. Leafs that float as birds do. Tree branches that are as antlers. But still, my hands cannot make the magic."

"Yes they can. Look, here is a stick. There is the sand of the cave floor. See, I use my hand to move the stick through the sand to make the shape of my other hand. And if it is wrong, then I brush the sand smooth and try again. If you do that enough, then you can do it with a blackened reed on the cave wall."

"Why are you teaching me this magic?"

"Because of all the young men I know, you are the one who asks the most questions, and that is the first part of magic. And because I trust you. And because someone else must learn to do this for the people."

"Why? Will you stop?"

"No. But I have known many more winters than you, and at sometime my spirit will be taken from me. Someone else will then have to do this magic. I think you are the one."

"I will try."

"I know. Now we must set the carved stones out on the great rock."

In the center of the chamber was a large flat rock, like a table. It had been dragged into the cave by many men many winters past. It was a deep red stone, unlike the creamy walls of the cave. Little veins of white shiny material ran though the red, so that the stone looked something like a huge slab of raw meat.

The older man pulled a deerskin bag out from under the rock, and carefully removed its contents. First was a bear claw to be used for the scarring. Then, wrapped in a piece of lioness hide, came the woman-stone.

She was of a soft yellow rock, shiny and smooth to the touch, and about as tall as a man's foot was long. Her head was a little featureless knob with a close-carved basket of hair. There was no neck. Her body curved like a fat pear down from the round shoulders, swelling past breasts like hanging gourds, then out to huge strong hips framing the extended globe of her belly, and all of these heavy rounded lines plunged down to that place where the man inserted his seed. Below, her legs, being of less use, dwindled to a stubby point. Everything about her surged to the making of babies.

"Will you teach me to make one of these?"

"Yes, but not with your eyes."

"How?"

By seeing with your fingers."

"How?"

"You have a woman. I have seen her."

"Yes."

"When you mate with her, do you close your eyes?"

"I don't remember."

"Sometimes you do."

"Maybe."

"And then you feel her. Her curves and softness."

"Yes."

"When you carve the stone, you remember that feeling of her. You close your eyes and touch the stone, and make the tips of your fingers into whole hands, and feel the curves. You carve and feel, and carve some more, and smooth the stone only when it is right, when you are sure that the woman's like-spirit is there."

"But once again, my hands..."

"Must be trained by working with softer things like the clay for making pots."

"Ah."

"Now place the point of her feet in that hole."

He gestured to one of two holes that had been drilled into the top of the great stone table. She stood there shining and oh-so round in the flickering torch light. Next the older man pulled a roll of stag-skin out of the bag.

"I do not like this. It feels broken." He said as he unrolled the skin. And he was right. The tube-shaped piece of dark stone was indeed broken. "We will have to hurry and make another. Come, and with the torch."

The younger man followed to small side chamber of the cave. Here was the older man's stock of pigments and bones, shells, and a collection of rocks. He rooted in the pile and found a slightly curved tusk, again about as long as a man's foot.

"We will make it from this."

"What is it?"

"Far to the west there is a great sea. One of the animals that lives in this sea has fur and a face like that of a young dog. It even makes a barking sound like the dog. But it is much bigger, and instead of legs and feet it has fins like a fish. This is one of its two big teeth."

"Have you been to the sea and seen this animal?"

"No, but those who travel and trade with me have. They brought me many of these stones and shells, and the long tooth."

"And what did you give them in return?"

"Carvings, like the woman and man-stones. And now we must make another man-stone. And fast. Come, I will show you how."

They returned to the main chamber with the tooth and the tools, and set them out on the stone table.

"Do you remember when you went through the man-spirit ceremony, three winters ago?" asked the older.

"Yes," replied the younger in a hushed voice.

"All of it?"

"Yes."

"Tell me."

"Why? You were there with me as my guide."

"Tell me."

"It was as cold then as it is now out there. All of the boys, seven of us, met their guides at the mouth of the cave. We went inside and felt the warm breath of the Earth's womb. We took off our cloaks and leggings so that we were naked."

"And then?"

"We marched, each boy and his guide, into the cave. You showed us the new paintings of the mammoths, and we all said prayers to bring them and all of the animals back. Then we sang the songs of the sprits."

"And next?"

"One the elders struck the drum, and one by one the guides took the bear claw and cut the mark on his boy's chest and stroked the ash in to make the scar happen. Here is mine."

"Mine has faded with age."

"But I see it still."

"Then what?"

"We stood in front of the table stone. And another of the elders took up the woman-stone and the man-stone and used them to dance the story of how life begins."

"And last?"

"We made a circle about the table stone."

"And?"

"And stroked ourselves, guides and new-men, stroked until, with the drum beating faster and faster, we..."

"Yes."

"...shot our seed on to the woman stone."

"All?"

The young one stopped and looked down at the cave floor and whispered his answer.

"No, not all. My seed hit the man-stone instead."

"Why?"

"I...do not know."

"I do. You were looking at all of the other new-men and guides. But you did not look at the woman-stone.

"No."

"I know this because my new-man ceremony was the same. I too spent my seed upon the man-stone."

"Oh."

"Perhaps that is why I want to teach you the magic ways."

He put the tusk on the table next to the two pieces of the broken man-stone.

"I made this broken stone. Made it as the like-spirit of my own. Stroked my self and felt and made the two alike."

The younger man was staring, first at the broken stone, then at his teacher, as the older stroked himself.

"See, they are alike, thick and straight."

The younger's heart was beating like the drum, and he was sweating too.

"But look at the tusk. It is longer, thinner, and it curves a bit."

The younger felt his own begin to swell.

"Now look down at yourself. They are the same. I will make this tusk into your like-spirit."

The younger's breath caught in his chest. Sweat beaded across it too.

The older looked down, took up one of the flint knives and began to carve the tip of the ivory.

"Now I must read the shapes."

He reached down and ran his fingertips lightly over the younger's glans. The silence roared. The younger stiffened even more. Not only down there but all of his body. And both men closed their eyes.

The older carved more, making the slit at the tip and bringing a groove down the bottom and up around on either side to the top, in order to make the collar of the glans. Then he felt the younger again with the same light touch of fingers. The younger stood very still and trembled, eyes closed, and breathing so slowly.

The older used a piece of soft stone to smooth the bell-shape and creases, then felt both the younger's tip and the ivory tip and smiled. The younger looked away. He stood there, tall and straight like a young tree, but beads of sweat ran down his flanks, and the hint of a sigh played upon his face.

Once again the older touched. This time his fingers ran along the bottom of the younger's penis, searching out the shape of the tube that ran there under the tight skin.

The younger trembled even more.

Now the bottom of the tusk was carved with two shallow parallel grooves to make the tube. Again the younger was touched, fingers running so lightly along the length, and then along the tusk, and last the smoothing. The older grasped the tusk with one hand and his model's penis with the other. He stroked both and heard the younger moan.

"Open your eyes."

He held the new man-stone out.

"It is done, but one thing more is needed. You must shoot your seed upon it for the final shine."

He reached up to let his fingers trail down the younger's chest, then through his bush of sandy hair, and finally stroked him. It only took a few strokes. And with a giant heaving gasp the younger covered the man-stone with his semen. Then the older took up a deerskin rag, smoothed the white juice into the new man-stone, and set it into the other hole drilled in the table stone. And it did shine.

"I will learn all the magic that you wish to teach me."

"I know."

"All of it."

"I know. That is why I came here two days ago and broke the other man-stone."

The younger's face relaxed into a quiet smile.

"Come, we must let the elders know that all is ready."

The two donned their leggings and cloaks, and left the Earth's womb to seek, further along the outcropping of the cliff, the dwellings of their people.

———

A very short time later, the spirits hiding deep within the earth's fissures must have been sore afraid of the shortest day, for they trembled and the earth shook. Then the crest of the cliff collapsed, and snow and rock roared down. We cannot guess how the painter or his pupil, or indeed their people, fared. But the Earth's womb was sealed away for twenty millennia.

During those long dark eons, water laced with calcium leeched through cracks that the earthquake had caused in the cavern's ceiling. It slowly dripped and evaporated leaving the residue of long stalactites, and below, the drips built up answering stalagmites.

In the Nineteen-fifties two stone masons, quarrying limestone blocks for a fireplace, uncovered an opening in the cliff face. Soon townspeople from nearby Figeac came with their electric torches to marvel at the painted animals. The archeologists followed, then the press, and finally the long impatient lines of tourists.

The woman-stone had been dislodged during the earthquake. She spent the twenty thousand years reclining in the mud of the cavern floor. She was discovered early on and today resides in a glass case in the provincial museum. The label reads "The Venus of Figeac." The broken man-stone was also found, still wrapped in its desiccated stag-skin sheath, but only accredited scholars are allowed to see it.

But the carved seal tusk stayed secure in its hole during the earthquake. High above a stalactite started to drip, encasing the ivory man-stone below in a white and glistening calcite cloak. The younger's like-spirit is still there on the slab of red porphyrite. But no one knows this. The tour guides, in passing, draw hurried attention to the stalagmite, so unusual in that this one had grown upward with a gentle curve.

A Boner Book

Alcibiades's Mirror

I can not savor fancy dishes such as braised tongue of peacock or eels stuffed with Persian figs. My stomach is delicate. Give me instead some well-cooked lamb with rice and grape leafs, a simple goat cheese and some watered wine. That is the reason why I always arrive both late and well-fed at the house of Maxagoras. His dinners are too rich, employing delicacies gathered from the far edges of the world by his captains. He owns Athens's largest merchant fleet. Indeed most of the grain that makes our city's daily bread, as well as the exports that pay for it, are transported in vessels owned by Maxagoras. He is the Croesus of our age.

Alas, I am only what one would call well off, but then my income is derived from a more limited market. I clothe athletes. Ah, you laugh, knowing that our athletes perform their wonders in the nude. Yet my products cover their bodies. First there is the matter of arriving for warm-ups at the palestrina. One's later nakedness is best revealed while discarding a well-cut chiton. My workshops make the best from fine Egyptian linens, worked with borders of gold-threaded frets, and cut as briefly as vanity might demand. Then there are the filets, which encircle each man's luxuriant curls as he parades out to the stadium. They too can be of gold, to say nothing of the victors' laurel wreaths.

I've cornered the market on those. Indeed, my workshop is the sole provider for awards at Olympia.

But my real income is derived from that which covers an athlete's nakedness—namely oil, and of all kinds. Maxagoras's ships bring them to me from every corner of the great sea. And camel caravans extend my reach to mystic capitals of unknowable eastern empires. A poor athlete must make do with ordinary olive oil: sticky, rancid and smelling of some farmer's nearby grove. But wealthy athletes...ah, they line my pockets for a finer sheen. Oils of thirteen kinds of palm, seven different nuts, two types of whale, and three of dolphin, as well as the most refined varieties of olive. I stock them all.

And I can delight them with scent. Attar of rose or lavender may be added to the oil for those men who wish to smell sweet at the end of a race. Cinnamon or clove can give one a bracing aroma. Ambergris, frankincense, and myrrh are more pungent still. There are also those who crave something, shall we say, in the super masculine vein? The addition of various musks of bear, ox, or a rare gazelle from Africa are said to drive an athlete's admirers to distraction.

Most important is the quality and color of the oil. After all, I am in the business of enhancing flesh. Would you like to look more ruddy? A touch of henna can be added to kiss your skin with sun. A golden glow? That's done with a distillate of saffron from Iberia. It is expensive, but oh-so-worth it. Something lighter? A fine-ground chalk will make your body as pale as pure marble. For the right price, we can glaze you with any color of the rainbow....

Then there's the sheen. For a glow that's soft as satin we'll employ the thinnest unguent, something that will soak into your skin. Nut oils are best. Ah, but you prefer to shine like polished marble? That demands a thicker viscosity. Olive, or better, bear oil will dazzle with the sharpest highlights. And we'll give it to you in a painted jar from Ceramica, or better, a vial of clear Syrian glass. Your own special blend. They'll go wild when you stride into the stadium.

There's more. Some utensils for application? Tweezers or fine razors to remove unsightly hair? Soft brushes to apply the oil? And of course a strigil to scrape it off. Do you prefer smooth wood, warm ivory or cool bronze? There's even a gold one that curves so nicely as it slides across your skin, and it only costs two hundred and fifty drachmas.

Ah, but enough of oil. I was telling you of Maxagoras's dinner party.

To begin, he lives in a veritable palace, and his dining room is spectacular. Marble shines everywhere. The round table is a polished slab of rosy alabaster, large enough in diameter that a tall man might spread-eagle himself upon it yet never reach the edge with toes and finger tips. I know this to be true for once a fetching youth, whose body was drenched in honey, had done precisely that as the grand finale of one of Maxagoras's dinners. Now there was a delicious spectacle!

Eight sumptuous couches surround this table, each wide enough for a guest to share with his boyfriend of the moment. Gilded bronze frames. Downy cushions. Covers of Persian silk. Even the servants are superb works of art. Maxagoras can afford to buy the handsomest of slaves. His flute boys delight with sinewy looks as well as sultry notes.

I arrived late, as I told you, dropping off some vials of Maxagoras's favorite oils. These were devised not only for looks, but for—how shall I put it? Ah yes, lubricative purposes. I left them with the porter and followed a servant into the dining room.

"Welcome, Lystrippus," said my host. "You know the others, but I don't think you've met Pietros."

The most gorgeous boy that I have ever seen—save one—smiled at me from Maxagoras's couch. He was tall, with the winnowy yet perfect proportions of a statue by the young Praxiteltes. Two gray-green eyes framed a chiseled nose. Tousled brown hair crowned a truly noble brow. High cheekbones waited impatiently for the first growth of a beard. Lips pouted as they smiled. And his skin had no need of any glow that I might add.

I almost stumbled back upon my couch, grateful for the extra cushions that my host had provided to accommodate a misshapen ancient back. Still, my eyes were glued to the vision of this winsome youth. But then my life has been spent with looking. In both business and pleasure I have been a happy voyeur imbibing visions of male beauty.

"Lystrippus foregoes the delights of my table, preferring food for thought," said our host while raising his cup for a toast, "so let us welcome him and hope that he will provide our dessert in the form of the topic for tonight's symposium."

"Ah no," said I, drinking with the rest. "An old man would rather hear the questions of the young." All of the other ephebes sharing couches looked up in horror. But the eyes of the most beautiful one glowed with anticipation, as I said: "I yield the choice of topic to Pietros."

He smiled with another perfect pout, then stood to ponder his choice while walking oh-so-gracefully around the table.

"My thanks, Lystrippus," said he in a voice as resonant as a young swan's trumpet. "We youths are here to learn both feeling and philosophy from our loving elders. We are in so many ways your willing receptacles. But I would have you consider another element of our instruction—the heroes of old. One in particular has been my favorite inspiration. I propose that you expound upon the mystery of Alcibiades."

Well now a gasp went round the room. Lysander, an old and respected Spartan general, practically choked upon his wine.

"How, boy, can you admire a man who played traitor to your city by coming over to our side, then betrayed us to serve the Persians, and yet again betrayed them to lead your fleet? I will never understand why your countrymen welcomed him back. Even at the end, he was assassinated while trying to raise yet another army of conquest in far off Thrace. You would honor the one man who most made it possible for Sparta to win and thereby rule Athens? Impossible."

"And yet," said Pietros with a smile, "you Spartans loved him...and followed his advice to win."

Now spoke Sardides, a wealthy wine dealer.

"Vainglorious. That's the word for Alcibiades. The man who you would make your hero trumped up the wild plans of empire that lost one Athenian army and a fleet in Sicily, and yet another fleet at Notrium to bankrupt our state. Only his ego was heroic.

"And yet you loved him. You chanted hymns upon the wharves and cheered the armies as they sailed."

Now it was the turn of Vanides, the most prosperous of our farmers.

"Ever grasping...selfish in the extreme, that was Alcibiades. I know of two men who sold their homes and all their goods to give him pleasure. And Hipponicus was so charmed that he gave Alcibiades the hand of his only daughter and then doubled the dowry."

"I have heard the histories of those men too," said Pietros, "and know that they went to their graves still loving him."

Even Maxagoras was abashed.

"My dear Pietros, would you make a god of one who profaned our gods. Impiety was Alcibiades second name. I am ashamed to admit that I myself was present at some of those infamous farragoes, during the days of the plague, when he dressed as Aphrodite and performed travesties of religion as a prelude to debauchery."

"Yet you loved him," said Pietros with a wicked smile, "and admitted to me that he taught you a sexual trick or two." He resumed his place beside Maxagoras.

Now the wisest man present, Plato, raised his voice..

"And Socrates loved him. It seems so long ago yet yesterday that Socrates was made to drink that cup of hemlock for the crime of 'corrupting the youth of Athens.' Perhaps Alcibiades was the prime example. But a love existed between them that was both deep and mutual."

Pietros said nothing, yet his eyes betrayed a greater glow. Then Maxagoras's hand wandered to the ephebe's thigh.

"So now," continued Plato, "let me, in the manner of my master, pose questions in search of answers. Young Pietros has provided the first query. Why, despite his treachery, impiety, avarice, and vanity did all of us love Alcibiades?

"His beauty was unexcelled," said Maxagoras. Pietros closed his eyes and removed the host's wandering hand, who sighed, adding, "and in the end, beauty excuses all."

I had to silently agree, for the one boy that I had known to surpass the beauty of this Pietros was a youth named Alcibiades.

Do you speak only of physical beauty, Maxagoras?" added Plato, "for did not Alcibiades himself find love in the ugly form of a squat and balding Socrates?

Now Pietros smiled ever-so sweetly at our paunchy host.

"There was more indeed to Alcibiades," answered Maxagoras, "for though he had a slight stammer, his voice could be both steel and honey."

"Oh, but it was his use of words that swayed our hearts," said Sardides. "He called forth cheers with ease. A regular Demonsthenes he was."

"And brilliant as a leader. Such unforeseen tactics," added Lysander. "The only way that I could defeat him was to hold back and refuse his bait. He was also skilled in the ways of loving ladies. Sparta's queen could tell you that. Our king was not amused."

"So could half the men here, if I am to believe Maxagoras," said Pietros, who received a reproving look from our host.

"And Socrates praised the beauty of his mind," said Plato. "So that now I must ask you to consider a new line of inquiry. Never was a man so truly blessed by the gods. I think we can all agree that Alcibiades had beauty of person, of mind, of voice, and of soul. But he was also the scion of a great lineage. Fortune blessed him with land and riches. Pericles was his guardian, Sparta his trainer, Athens his teacher, and Socrates his mentor. So now we must consider the greatest mystery—why should such a lucky man turn thrice traitor to all who loved him?"

A long silence reigned here.

It was my turn. "Perhaps, dear Plato, we should ask a different question. There is an old saying. 'What does one give the man who has everything?' I would ask what Alcibiades wanted more than anything in the world.

"And you would answer?" said Pietros, raising up from his couch on one arm, his eyes burning into mine.

"I too shall be Socratic and answer with yet another question. Pietros, I offer this question above all to you—without a mirror, can Narcissus still exist?"

"Who, Lystrippus, is your Narcissus?" Said the young man, "Alcibiades...or me?"

"I think all beautiful men are forced to be Narcissus. That is their curse. They cannot help being the happy accidents of birth. Nor can they easily avoid the special looks of envious others."

"Alas, that is so."

"And thus at length, such lucky, or unlucky men as the case might be, must need to see themselves. To see the miracle that makes others smile, sigh, love, covet and even conspire."

"Ah, you have hit it, wise Lystrippus."

"And yet, fair Pietros, the reaction is the same for someone as misshapen as myself. The time comes when the horrified looks, or worse, turning askance of others, drives the ugly man to search out a reflection."

"I have not looked away from you."

"No, Pietros, you have not, but perhaps there is a beauty in your soul as well as form. Yet we all at some time must see what other see in us, hence the value of a mirror."

"But such reflections are rare and fleeting," said Pietros. "Still waters are too easily ruffled by light breezes. Narcissus must have been a frustrated lad."

"Then how unfortunate," interjected Plato, "that our artisans have fallen so short in the invention of a fine reflective surface."

"That is true," added Maxagoras, "These poor little bronze mirrors of ours show a face but dimly."

"Which is precisely," said I, "why I long ago secretly engaged the finest of artisans to solve the problem. Oh not because I wished to view myself, though I have and am mercifully cured, but because my business dictates that I allow handsome men to see themselves burnished by my oils."

"But we were discussing the mystery of Alcibiades," grumbled Lysander, "not Narcissus's mirror."

"Patience gentlemen," said I. "The answer to both ciphers may be found in a perfect mirror, which in turn depends upon secrets of fine grinding and the presence of a remarkable metal.

"Those poor little mirrors that you rightfully despise, Maxagoras, are made by placing a bronze disc beneath a long metal bar that is suspended from a point a man's height above. Different abrasives are attached to end of the bar, and as it swings back and forth across the plate, as smooth surface is polished in the shape of a section of a sphere. That curved surface is what makes the mirror seem to enlarge your face."

"Come, come, Lystrippus," whined the wine dealer. "We are far afield from our topic."

"Again, bear with me, and I promise you that the form of Alcibiades will play the greater part in the...body...of my story.

"The use of the long bar is important because it is rigid and fixed in its radius, thus ensuring a perfect polished surface, albeit curved. But therein hangs the problem. We might lengthen the bar tremendously, and suspend it, say, if the Archon would allow, from the highest point in the Parthenon. But still the mirror would be curved, if more gently. It would still magnify. But I needed a large flat mirror that would reflect all of a man's body at true size.

"My artisans, the gods bless them, came up with a solution involving a bar of Hittite iron that slides back and forth on two tracks of the same metal. Now the problem was what surface. We tried silver from the mines at Laurium but it was too soft to hold the flat shape and take a smooth polish. Gold was worse, and who, aside from our host, could afford it? Alas bronze would have to do, for I wanted this mirror to be large...at least the size of a warrior's shield.

"Well, we did it. Ground it. Polished it. Mounted it in a strong and handsome frame. And were dismayed, like you Maxagoras, at the darkness of the image. One peered to see one's self in a sea of Stygian gloom. We should have carved the frame with the figure of Charon and his boat. This was not the way to sell athletes on the benefits of an oil's healthy glow.

"That was when I heard tales of a magic substance called 'quick silver.' It may be heated to ooze out of an Iberian rock named 'cinnabar.' My dear friend, our host, obtained it for me. But this is the remarkable quality: the little silvery droplets may be smoothed out upon the flat bronze plaque to provide a mirror as bright and clear as day. It will not last, turning powdery red when the weather turns wet, but new applications will restore the shine many times.

"Hooray! I had invented the perfect sales tool. I mounted my mirror and its frame in a little wagon, like a box, lined with black cloth and lit by an overhead opening to the bright sun. Thus might an athlete might enter, close the door, witness my oils spread upon his skin, and see clearly, for the first time, exactly what others saw in the glory of his face and body.

"My mirror and wagon were ready in time for the three hundred and forty fourth Olympiad. That may seem long ago, Pietros—more than three decades—but that year Alcibiades would make his first appearance at the games, and he, sprouting the beginning of a beard, was but little older than you are today."

Pietros blushed and brought one hand up to stroke his smooth cheek.

"Now, let me tell you of another of Alcibiades's triumphs, and one that he had achieved even at your tender age. That boy had become the arbiter of Athenian fashion. When, thinking it too effeminate, he declined to study flute in favor of the Lyre, why then two score flute teachers went on the dole and lyres sold out in every music shop. When Alcibiades declared in favor of a certain kind of sandal, soon all of the other young men of Athens called the sandal by his name and knew that they must have a pair. I knew my business, gentlemen. I'm sure that you can understand why I decided to keep my mirror a secret until such time as Alcibiades might celebrate its premier.

"I took my cart and wagons full of oils on the long journey to Olympia, set up my booth near the Palestrina, and sent a servant with a special invitation to the tent of Alcibiades. He arrived the next noon, with four friends in attendance. A crowd followed to watch them enter my booth. Fortune was smiling on me.

"Ah my friends, you should have seen him—a body smoother and more graceful than the *Discolobus* of Myron. More well proportioned than the perfect dream of Polycleitus's *Canon*. And a face that outshone the *Hermes* of Praxiteles. No—better—fair Helen may be no more than Homer's misty myth, but history knows that Alcibiades truly had the face that launched, and led, and alas, lost a thousand ships."

My voice faltered here, and Pietros warmed my heart by bringing his goblet over and raising it to my lips. Then he composed himself on the floor at the foot of my couch.

Maxagoras frowned, but I spoke on.

"My usual practice with an important customer was to demonstrate the products on the bodies on one of four slaves purchased for their perfection and skin tones varying from darkest bronze to palest white. I chose the one closest in complexion to Alcibiades and began applying the different oils. He added the torsos of his four friends into the bargain, and soon the whole range of sheens, scents, and shades was on display.

"He decided upon a tasteful sheen this side of shiny—oil of a Tuscan olive leavened with a touch of almond. The color was a light golden copper— with a smidgen of henna and another of saffron. And the scent? I cannot describe it, but his nose was also talented. Some grains of cinnamon, a whiff of ambergris, and a few drops of the gazelle musk—an aroma to match the sensuality of his face. We mixed enough for one application and served it up in a Syrian vial warmed to the liking of his touch.

"I gave the vial to Alcibiades and led him to the mirror chamber, ushered him in and closed the door. Then I pulled the line that opened the skylight, and drew back another curtain to reveal the mirror. Alcibiades was transfixed by his own life-size reflection when I withdrew.

"Outside I set some of my associates to the serving of his friends. Others saw to the mixing of four additional vials of Alcibiades's oil. When all were busied, I disappeared around the corner of the mirror wagon to enter a secret door in its far side, for here, through holes cleverly carved into the frame, I could indulge my voyeur's passion."

Lysander spit out his wine again. "Does that mean, Lystrippus, that you spied on me years ago when I used your magic mirror?"

"You'll never know, Lysander. I shall not speak of those who live."

"Then, by all the gods, I'll do my best to outlive you!"

Pietros began to giggle.

"And luck be with you, Lysander," said I, while giving the boy a swift but subtle kick.

"But what did you see?" asked Pietros, pressing his hand upon my knee, and speaking in a throaty voice that could not be denied.

"I saw love—deepest love. Alcibiades had shed his chiton and his sandals. He stared forward at the mirror, turning his nude body this way and that, angling himself to see his back, the curve of his calves and thighs, the long fine fullness of his arms, as he slowly raised them, reaching to the sun. He never took his eyes off of the mirror. It was as though he was discovering himself. He used his hands to feel his face, trace the cords of his neck, slide over his shoulders, run down across his chest, tweaking his nipples. and then kneading the ridges of his stomach. His hands floated down along the sculpted ridges of his belly, smoothed the contours of his thighs and calves, then one hand reached down for the vial.

"He raised it to the sun and for the first time took his eyes from the mirror to observe the oil's amber glow. His breathing grew heavier and his nether member thickened and pulsed. Then he turned the vial to drip the liquid over his shoulders and along his upper chest. Now he watched the mirror again as the oil ran down in golden rivulets across his pectorals, and along the grooves of his abdominals. He poured more to watch it ooze through pubic hair, and down along his thighs."

Pietros seemed to shudder against my leg. I continued in a quiet voice not quite my own, for in truth, I had never told anyone this tale.

"Then Alcibiades began to use his hands to spread the oil. Breathing harder as he smoothed it over his shoulders and arms. Sighing as he used it to glaze the planes of his chest and stomach. Almost purring as he reached down to spread it over one leg and then the other, never taking his eyes away from the mirror. Then his penis began to rise, and he gasped as his hand stroked down across his belly, through the hair, and finally oozed the oil along his member, so rigid now, pointing higher and higher.

"Soon he was moaning, humming some urgent wordless song as he arched his back and let the sun play in dancing highlights on the rigid cords of muscle, while one hand floated up and down along his ribs, and the other stroked his penis."

In truth the dining room had seemed to vanish. My old eyes saw only a young Alcibiades, perfect as a dream, a golden statue humming like a lyre string, rigid yet throbbing, transfixed with his own image. Even now, in the midst of my eighth decade, I felt strong stirrings below at the memory of then, of erupting without touching myself, while beyond the mirror of my memory he exploded at the wonder of his own reflection.

I must have ceased speaking, for suddenly Pietros was kneeling, tugging at my sleeve.

"Lystrippus, would you like to rest? Another sip of wine?"

The room came back into focus. So did the wide-eyed faces of all the guests.

"I...I beg your pardons. I have gone beyond the bonds of..."

"No, Lystrippus," said Plato, in a quiet, even voice, "you have given us a vivid, living portrait of Alcibiades. What happened next?"

"Yes," said Pietros, sitting beside me now while Maxagoras fumed from his couch across the room, "Tell us."

I took a sip of wine and resumed the tale.

"I hurriedly rearranged my hymation to a semblance of respectability and scurried out to 'oversee' my workers so that I was there when Alcibiades emerged, radiant in one if our briefest chitons and a new pair of gilded sandals. He stepped down from the wagon and turned and twirled to the applause of his friends.

" 'Make that six vials, Lystrippus,' he said, 'and show me what you stock in the way of strigils.'

"Alcibiades, true to his manner and resources, purchased one or two of the best of everything that I offered, including two of the expensive gold strigils. Then his friends stepped to the fore, each desiring a vial of the same oil mixture, whereupon Alcibiades called me aside with a request that we keep the formula for the scent as a secret only for his use. And I, sensing the inestimable value of exclusivity, happily agreed.

"My fortune was made. That season we could not keep up with the demand for <u>Oil of Alcibiades</u>."

"You sold me several vials," laughed Lysander, "and that was two years later."

"We still sell it," laughed I, "but I have more to tell you of Alcibiades and the mirror. That afternoon he ran his first race. He did not win, and therefore was not crowned with one of my golden wreaths, but all spoke in wonder of his appearance. He conquered the crowd with ease."

"That's the story of his life," grumbled Lysander, "magnificent entrances and shoddy exits."

"The next day, wearing a dark hood, he came alone via a back route to my booth. 'I would use your mirror again, Lystrippus, to ensure that the oil is applied correctly. My servants are all such dolts.' 'Of course,' said I. This routine was carried on for the length of his stay in Olympia. I watched as much as I could, but business was brisk and often kept me at the counter.

"Two months later I returned to Athens, and soon knocking at my door was Alcibiades in the company of a comely slave as young as you, Pietros, and almost as fair. Alcibiades bought two vials of the oil, and with a wink to me, ushered his servant into the mirror chamber, which was now installed in the back of my shop. I locked my outer door and hastened to the secret one, thinking to watch our hero play the grown man's part. He did but with a twist.

"Alcibiades stood naked with his legs and arms spread wide, in the form of an X, while the servant donned a black, long-sleeved, hooded Persian tunic, leaving only his hands visible. He stood behind, pouring the oil, reaching around, allowing his master the illusion that disembodied hands smoothed the oil on his body. Oh did both Alcibiades and I enjoy this spectacle, so much so that once again we both spewed our seed in unison. Only Alcibiades shot his into the face of the slave, and I into the empty darkness of a secret room.

"Shortly after his servant appeared again to hand me a note requesting another vial of oil. That was when I realized that the lad could not speak, indeed had lost his tongue. Alcibiades's reflective visits with his mute attendant continued for the next two years or so. Of course I watched as many times as possible.

"Then two older citizens knocked on my door. It was those two you mentioned earlier, Vanides. They offered me a fortune for the mirror as a gift for Alcibiades, an offer so lucrative that I could not refuse, for I did not know then that they had mortgaged their homes and goods to raise the money. I would not miss the mirror in terms of business. My name had come to mean enough. I did miss the secret shows however. But now Narcissus had his mirror."

"He did not bring it to Sparta," said Lysander, "for he was watched by a whole cadre of spies. I had agents in his household, and would have known."

"You are correct, Lysander. But Alcibiades did take the mirror and the mute aboard his galley for the Sicilian campaign. I know this because his servant purchased oils and a bottle of the quicksilver just before the fleet's departure. Two months later another galley was dispatched with orders for Alcibiades's arrest and arraignment here in Athens on those charges of impiety. We all know how he fled alone and secretly. The mirror and the mute were abandoned. No more was heard of them—lost, like an army and a fleet. And without his mirror, so, think I, was Alcibiades lost."

"Come, come, my friend," said a weary Plato, for the night was late and the oil lamps were beginning to sputter. "Beware the facile explanation. The simple loss of a mirror cannot explain the complexity of multiple betrayals." "You are correct, of course, Plato. But think on this:

> 'We men love beauty in the boy,
> Yet see our friends grow gray and gaunt.
> That beauty gives us fleeting joy.
> For now we know how time doth haunt.'

"Imagine that the most beautiful thing you know, that which gives you the greatest pleasure and is the utmost object of your love, is your own form and face. But with maturity come changes. You can see the skin weather on your legs and arms. You can feel the battle scar on your back. But without a mirror you cannot see your face, and finger tips will poorly read its coming creases.

"You try to find reflections in other ways. Yet the painters and sculptors work too slowly. Besides, their skill is too often tempered with flattery, and it cannot live. Soon you search out lovers' eyes, wallowing, for example, in the embraces of a Spartan queen. But perhaps, and forgive me in this, Lysander, perhaps the Spartan mirror is too stern and dark, like tarnished bronze. So you seek out warmer, brighter reflections in the misty sheen of Persian silks. And then, as youthful dreams grow hazy and you discover some gray hairs upon your silken pillow, Athens, brave city of your youth, calls you back unto her bosom.

"The day after his victorious fleet had docked at Piraeus, Alcibiades appeared at my shop. He still dazzled, but the bloom of youth had been superceded by a more haggard handsomeness."

"Your mirror, Lystrippus, I would purchase it."

" But you already have."

"Your replacement then."

"There is none. No need, Alcibiades. Your fame guaranteed mine."

"Then have another made and hang the cost."

Lysander exploded: "This at a time when he was penniless and the payment of his fleet was in arrears! You greedy man."

"But, Lysander, I refused his request. Besides those artisans had long ago perished with our army, and the wars had cut off traffic with Iberia.

"That was the last time that I saw him. Within a few months you, Lysander, had destroyed our fleet, and Alcibiades had fled Athens under yet another indictment. After he had slammed my door, one of my workers parted the curtains at the back of the shop and mimed, "Is he gone?" I nodded, and Alcibiades's mute came forward. Both he and the mirror had survived the Sicilian captivity. I, with the help of one our host's captains, had seen to their rescue. That was how I learned that the mute had lost his tongue at the command of Alcibiades. And I knew then that I would never again contribute to Narcissus's cause. The mute has been my most trusted associate.

Indeed, he is my heir."

One oil lamp still lingered as the guests look their leave. I lurched my way home through a gloomy night, fell into my bed, and slept heedless of the world 'til noon of the next day, waking to the sound of knocking on the shop door.

"Yes, yes, I'm coming down."

It was Pietros.

"I am given to understand that one may purchase the Oil of Alcibiades here."

"You are correct, young man," said I with a bow as I ushered him in.

"Then I would have one vial. And with, if it be possible, the addition of the secret scents."

"Of course."

He waited patiently while I mixed and warmed.

"A vial of the Syrian glass?"

"Of course. I can pay you well."

"Ah, but this shall be my gift."

"Then I will be bold and ask for one thing more."

"You have only to name it."

"I have heard tales of a remarkable mirror. Might I see it?"

"This way, young patron."

I led him back through the curtain to the workroom, past lines of amphora and vast copper vats, past bottles of spices and jars of tinctures, to a dim corridor that led to a bolted door. It opened on a dark and musty room.

But when the widow curtains were withdrawn to admit a golden beam of light, and when the surface was dusted and new quicksilver smoothed upon the bronze, there stood the mirror in all its glory.

I bowed and backed towards the door.

"No need, Lystrippus, to scurry to your secret chamber. Stay here and be another mirror."

Reader, an old man thanked the gods. And stayed.

The Last Roman God

The Pantheon squats in the middle of Rome like an ancient toad. Having long ago shed a sleek marble skin to satisfy the greed of Renaissance princes and popes, the temple's outer aspect is now gouged and stained with the warts of two millennia. A raw concrete dome, stripped of bronze sheathing by the same popes, looms as the toad's humped back. And the once welcoming portico—eight columns gaunt with grime and a dark pediment shorn of decorative friezes—today resembles a gaping maw eager to swallow human flies.

But once swallowed, the modern tourist is astounded by one of the triumphs of architecture. The dome's interior soars one hundred and forty-two feet to form a coffered hemisphere as perfect as the heavens. At the apex is an immense open oculus, through which a palpable column of morning sunlight rams down to reveal the features of the western wall. Then this searing beam drives through the day across a time-scarred marble floor to burn its way back up the eastern wall.

As it sweeps, the giant sundial reveals many niches lining the lower drum. They were the building's original marvels, having been created to display images of that which gave the temple its name: "all of the gods." During the Second Century the Emperor Hadrian constructed the Pantheon to acknowledge the religions not only of Rome, but Greece and Gaul, Egypt and Ethiopia, Persia and Parthia, in short of every imperial province. Later gods also found a place. Heroes and Caesars had been deified by the Senate. Even an obscure sect known as the Christians was invited to include an image of their new deity, but being in thrall to the stern words of their First Commandment, the offer was refused. Nonetheless, the true glory of the Pantheon was to serve as history's foremost monument to religious tolerance.

Two centuries later the Christians had clawed their way to dominance. "Thou shalt have no other God before me," shouted that initial commandment. With tolerance no longer a valid consideration, the Pantheon was consecrated as a church, and its now 'pagan' statues torn from their pedestals and niches. Many shattered as they crashed down to the floor. All were hauled away for rubble. The very first figure to be toppled was one of the last to have been set up in the temple of all the gods. The mob growled with vengeful triumph as fragile alabaster smashed into a thousand pieces. It had been the image of an incredibly beautiful youth.

Two hundred miles south of the delta, the River of Rivers was a wide band of mud-laden water, slow but relentless in its glassy march to the sea. So smooth, in fact, that of an October night in the eleventh year of Hadrian's reign, and the fifty-third of his life, the Nile formed a broad and murky mirror. Above were a million sparks of light as the Milky Way splashed across the heavens like an extravagant diamond necklace. The same diamonds shimmered as reflections in the river's tarnished darkness. On the near shore, another group of fuzzier white dots bobbed while lapping the river's life-giving water. But the shepherd who guarded this flock of thirsty sheep and goats gazed with wonder at a fantastic apparition gliding upstream. A quartet of Roman triremes accompanied the Emperor's barge for a state visit to explore the even then ancient wonders of Egypt.

A fine breeze had welled up from the North, thus five huge sails billowed above like striped clouds, and triple ranks of oars had been locked in their raised position, giving the five ships the aspect of great birds, lumbering upstream while drying their wings. Below decks, galley slaves slept on or beneath their rude wood benches, while soldiers snored more comfortably in hammocks hung between the staves. On deck only a few crewmen could be seen. Lookouts fought sleep in each bow, scanning for occasional floating tree trunks, carcasses, or other flotsam. Aft, helmsmen and their helpers watched the sails and managed the giant steering oars. And on the Emperor's barge three musicians huddled at the bottom of the mast. A drummer, a flutist and a lyre player provided lilting Greek melodies that warbled over the water and sounded most exotic to the shore-bound Egyptian shepherd.

His eyes were drawn to a small pavilion that glowed amidships on the far off barge. Slender silver columns held up a silken canopy, and gossamer curtains wafted as its walls. Many oil lamps burned within like a miniature golden Milky Way. And there were moving shadows: the sinuous shapes of a dancing naked youth.

Onboard, during those moments when the music ebbed, the crewmen sometimes heard a low rumble but no distinct words. It was the entranced threnody of the Emperor's voice.

"It is heaven to watch you dance, Antinous, to see the light caress your body, to witness the divine music of your movements."

Antinous smiled, as he always did, shy and silent, eyes closed, pleased that Hadrian was pleased, but more pleased that dancing stirred cooling breezes. His body shined from unguents purchased in Athens. The Emperor had so enjoyed smoothing the perfumed oils into Antinous's skin as they sprawled on silken cushions. That smoothing had felt good, so very good, but oil grew sticky with underlying sweat in the heat of Egypt. Breezes cooled. Dancing with lazy movements to the languid rhythms strummed by the hired musicians cooled even more.

"All of those statues that we bought in Athens, those athletes and gods, those Hermes and Apollos, have great beauty. Even better are the two bronzes I had made of you. Sometimes I slip down to the hold and run my finger tips across their sculpted bodies, but I would rather let my eyes caress your living flesh, Antinous."

More silent smiling as the eighteen-year-old twirled in the soft breeze, all the while thinking of Bithynia, the home that Hadrian had spirited him away from five years ago, and of cooler winds blowing over rolling northern Anatolian hills. He might dance forever with that happy thought, but knew that his master would soon want to caress flesh with more than eyes.

"Tomorrow we will dock at Abydos, where the god Osiris died and was reborn. A stirring tale of resurrection. The Egyptians believe that his goddess sister found his dismembered body floating in the Nile, gathered up his parts, joined them and then through heavenly magic made him live again forever. Resurrection is one way to become a god."

Antinous spun around, looking up through impossibly long lashes, and his gray-green eyes seemed to ask if there might be other ways

"Godhood may also be achieved through election by the Senate. But that usually depends upon bribes and bullying, and the results are chancy. Many an old emperor-god's temple is now decaying and forgotten."

Antinous danced closer. Hadrian reclined upon the cushions. Such perfection swayed before his eyes. The boy's mop of golden hair. His high cheek bones and pouting lips. A corded neck and finely chiseled torso. Firm round arms, and graceful hands that seemed somehow to speak. Hips that moved with such entrancing invitation. Legs like supple columns. And feet that were springing ribbons of grace.

"Or, Antinous, divinity might be just the act of being you."

The dancer towered, the light from myriad lamps glinting on his burnished flesh.

"They say that when a new god is created a new star will shine in the heavens."

Antinous twisted and arched his body, letting starry highlights play across his chest and groin. Hadrian sank more deeply into the cushions and sighed with anticipation.

"The Christians believe that their god was resurrected. It really is the more effective way to godhood. A leader dies. Some think they see him afterward. Then rumors of afterlife spread to make the new god live."

Antinous's eyes registered a lidded look of doubt.

"Ah, how fine it would to be able to believe such tales. But I do like an opinion that their god is reputed to have had."

A sideways look, with eyebrows arched in mild interest.

"When asked of taxes, he said 'Render unto Caesar that which is Caesar's, and unto God that which is God's'. Good for him. Makes life easier for my tax collectors."

Antinous smiled and spun so that the golden orbs of his buttocks might delight the Emperor. Hadrian sat up and reached out to cup the satin cheeks.

"And now, Antinous, <u>you</u> must render unto Caesar."

The dancer slowed his swaying, and felt his master rise, felt hands glide along his flanks, then lightly circle round to play upon his chest...stubby soldier's hands bedecked with jeweled rings. Next Antinous felt Hadrian's beard rub against his neck.

"You render unto me, and I...will render you."

Then the Emperor entered him.

One must not think that Antinous was mute or lacked intelligence. It was just that he had long ago realized that an imperial court could be very dangerous place. Hadrian's wife, ignored and childless, was a bitter, vengeful soul. Senators and generals schemed beyond every corner. Even servants plotted. It was better to say little, and do less, to be unaccounted, indeed to be a cipher. Antinous was content to be his emperor's faithful puppy, listening, lapping, loving, being groomed and petted, and asking for nothing in return. So much safer as a cipher.

Although the sailors had been carefully instructed to look everywhere but at the gossamer pavilion, the musicians made frequent sidelong glances. They had to, in order to take their cues. Dancing had ceased. New music was called for: slower, more insinuating tunes. Greek lullabies of love.

Seed spent, the Emperor and his paramour lolled conjoined upon the cushions, as was Hadrian's constant whim; the imperial ram so to speak yet embedded in the captive pleasure craft. Antinous, cupped within his master's hirsute embrace, felt the beard rasp along his neck as the voice droned on.

"And now, you might ask why of late I talk of gods. After all, an Emperor owns the world. I send out armies and change boundaries at will. I gather taxes and build wonders. I can change the course of rivers. I have the ultimate power of life and death.

"I even have you.

"There is only one thing beyond my control, one aspect of existence that only gods may manage, and that is time. My age is three times yours. While my own body begins to weaken I sheathe myself in your youth. My bones creak as yours grow strong. My face creases while yours glows smooth as alabaster. And my muscles wither, while yours...ah, yours...

"True gods, being immortal, stop time. They even, if the legends be true, may be able to reverse it on occasion. An ability, alas, denied to emperors."

Hadrian's ram had shriveled now and slipped out of the captive craft's hull, but his hands, like sailors' boarding parties, explored the decks, playing across Antinous's chest and neck and face.

"Time touches you as well and paints you with ever more beauty, such exquisite beauty, but it also brings forth the one thing that must drive us apart. Oh, I know that you have secretly begun to pluck and shave, but I still feel the hard stubble budding on your cheek and the fuzz of your chest begin to stiffen into body hair. And we both know that the world will frown upon any citizen, even an emperor, who dallies with a boy become a man. Alas, gossip is also beyond an emperor's control.

"Oh to be a god, to be able to silence tongues and freeze time to a year or so ago."

Youth dreamed only of one tongue's silence. Oh to hear Hadrian's snore, to be able to slip away and thereby banish stickiness with a cooling swim.

"When I die some years hence and become a god, Antinous, I will first appear to you."

Antinous took one of the Emperor's engulfing hands, kissed it and murmured, "And I to you."

"Thank you, yet surely I am the one who will succumb first. But I will not immediately set time back. Not until you and others have had time to spread the tales of my resurrection. And then I'll...Ah, but I feel the stirrings of another kind of resurrection..."

Youth sighed in resignation as invigorated age re-entered.

―――――――――

Much sand had run through the helmsmen's glass before the musicians heard the Emperor's snores and drifted off to their own happy sleep. The sailors kept their eyes aloft, for the wind was weakening. The great sail had begun to luff and slap against the mast. At any moment they would have to awaken the rowers to take up the slack. Thus no one saw Antinous slide free of Hadrian's arms, then use a strigil to try to scrape the oil away. Nor did they notice when he left the pavilion and climbed over the rail of the barge. And the first great boom of the oar-master's drum covered the sound of a splash as Antinous dove headfirst into the blessed inky coolness.

Eight slow drumbeats started the vast human machine of a trireme. During the first six beats the three superimposed ranks of three rowers per bench unlocked each of one hundred and twenty oars and ran them out in splendid unison. The last two gave the downbeat.

Antinous swam deep alongside the ship. He had done this many times while under sail, and being strong and fast, had always been able to keep up. Oh, how good the cold water felt. At last, having expelled a final bubble, he surged to the surface, to gasp for new air. That was when one of the giant oaken paddles crashed down upon his neck, broke it, and drove him back into the depths. The lifeless body surfaced again only to be smashed by several oars of the following trireme. That helmsman had heard sodden thumps and looked aft to see yet another carcass bobbing off to darkness in the murky wake. Some poor calf or deer, thought he as the ship glided on into the starry Nile night.

***

The ambrosia of Antinous had bequeathed to Hadrian deep sleep and oh-such-pleasant dreams. He awoke as the barge hove to at Abydos to find his arms curled around a cushion. The dear boy must be on deck, up in the bow, enjoying the sights. The Emperor adjusted his tunic and strode forth into a bright morning of cooler breezes and a parting wave of courtly bows. But where was Antinous? No gangway had been lowered. The forward watchman had seen no one swim ashore. Had the boy gone below? Cook had not seen him, nor any of the centurions. Hadrian even visited the hold, hoping to glimpse a living statue in the shadows, but found only shrouded bronze and marble

Three days later, after two of the triremes had been dispatched to search the shores downstream, and mounted troops had spread word in every riverside village, the same shepherd of that previous starlit night once more led his flock to drink. Something bloated and pasty-white bobbed among the entangling reeds. Possibly a drowned pig, thought the shepherd as he waded out. Then he saw blackened bruises and puffy face, and realized that this poor horrid thing might be the Greek boy that the soldiers sought. He was right. Others from his village held wine-soaked rags to their noses as they helped him drag the putrid carcass to their little temple. One villager rode off upon a bedraggled camel to tell the soldiers.

That night the citizens gaped as a grand chariot and a century of roman soldiers marched into their village square. The stern troops drew a cordon round the temple, and the Emperor, with leaden steps, went in alone. All heard the long and anguished cry and stood there wide-eyed as the dying wails echoed among the mud walls of their huts. After a long while a gaunt and haunted Hadrian emerged, conferred briefly with a contingent of Egyptian priests, and then savagely lashed his horses as he raced back to his camp. As experts at the restorative techniques of pharonic taxidermy, the priests would, several weeks later, send a large, richly carved, lead-lined cedar chest to the Emperor's barge at Alexandria.

Hadrian spent those same weeks hoping, praying with all of his jaded heart, for signs of resurrection. A soldier, swimming in the buff, emerged from the Nile to look for one moonlit moment like Antinous. Then he turned and trudged up the bank to join his comrades at a bivouac bonfire. Clouds swirled overhead in ways that, for an instant, resembled the boy's glorious mop of hair. Smoke danced above the braziers in the Emperor's tent with twirling wisps that sorely tantalized. Each evening Hadrian scanned every sector of the sky hoping to see a new star. His court astrologers joined him. But their charts always had an explanation for each fresh-seeming glint of light. Even dreams proved to be barren messengers, and many were horrid nightmares of a bruised and bloated face.

But there were other, more prosaic means to make a god. Hadrian instructed his engineers to lay waste to the village and plan a new city to be called Antinouopolis. Its temple must be a future wonder of the world. And to Hades with the original inhabitants. Proper Greek citizens would be recruited from Alexandria.

A month later the Emperor sailed for Greece. Athenian marble carvers and bronze casters rode to happy prosperity with many requests for statues of the new god. Temples sprouted everywhere that Hadrian's fleet dropped anchor. Bythinian citizens found themselves delighted to worship at sanctuaries dedicated to a native son. Coins were minted to place the divine image of Antinous in every citizen's palm.

On the return cruise to Rome, one trireme was detached to Athens with orders to bring the best of her sculptors to Rome. He did not go willingly, but a Roman short sword can be a most effective persuader.

Rome herself proved more resistant to Hadrian's new theology, but eventually bribes and bullying met with Senatorial success. The cedar chest was interred with great pomp at the Emperor's villa, but not before the Greek sculptor had joined the Emperor for a last long sighing look at priestly handiwork. Then Hadrian took the artist aside to examine a large block of perfect golden alabaster.

Several thousand statues of Antinous had been created. Fine tawny marbles or glistening bronze were the usual media. But Alabaster, being translucent, allowed for a final trick of godhood. The new statue was designed for a special niche at the Pantheon. Three hollows were carved at the back of the head, torso and groin, wherein hidden oil lamps might glow for an eternity guaranteed by priestly care. Thus, even at night, when only the moon's cool glow filtered down from the oculus, the image of Antinous would dazzle with god-like golden brilliance.

Hadrian, visiting the Pantheon during such a moonlit night was well pleased. The old Emperor could almost believe in his new god.

Saladin's Loom

I sing a song of warriors' tents,
Of the Lion and the Lamb,
Of a casket and a chilled peach,
And how peace came to our land.

Praise be to Allah, I am no poet—only a simple physician's assistant. The simplicity is mine alone. My master, a physician called Abondec al-Hakim, is foremost in the world of medicine, possessing so great a fame that he is often called upon to minister to the needs of the Supreme Sultan.

I measure and mix elixirs of the physician's devising. I inventory his stores and scribe the records of his diagnoses. I love and learn from his wisdom. So strong is my love that I even care for his camels. Indeed, I kiss al-Hakim's feet with thanks for my new life.

My former service was in the establishment of Abad ibn-Aman, who maintained the finest house of houris in Jerusalem. He was rich, and grew richer still with the realization that a stable of comely youths might add even more dinars to his coffers, for though the Prophet's words decry the love of men for boys, yet sometimes in His wisdom Allah will wink and look aside.

My former life was not unpleasant. A beautiful boy is pampered by his master, for being prized by patrons. And even now at the age of one and twenty, have I the sinewy figure, the smooth skin and the long hair of silken sheen that is desired by many men. My one complaint came in the forms and faces of the patrons. Men of wealth seldom stir one's heart, and thus would I find that the talents of an actor must too often supercede the skills of the body. Such performances soon became most tiresome.

One day, al-Hakim came to my chamber, a visit which was to eliminate all need for an actor's skill. It was not his visage that entranced me, for his age is more than three times mine, and his face is much weathered by experience. But his soul was beautiful, and it shined through his hands—a physician's hands that knew nooks and crevices and many other points of sensuous pleasure—in short, Dear Reader, he could knead my needs in ways I did not know that I could need. And thus made me need him, for the unique act of finding his pleasure in mine.

On a later day, Abondec al-Hakim paid many Dinars to Abad ibn-Aman for the privilege of my constant service. And though I can no longer say that I am pampered, yet every time the muezzin sings out from his minaret I give thanks to Allah for my new station.

Now, at the mid-point of my new apprenticeship, would our little caravan sail westward from Jerusalem through vast sandy seas to seek the sultan's encampment somewhere west of Jaffa. Al-Hakim led our progress from his perch on the back of the first camel, which also bore the leather boxes of his instruments. I sat bestride the hump of the second ship of the dessert, who carried the cases of our pharmacopoeia. The last was riderless, yet this beast traveled under the most important burden of all—my master's library—boxes of scrolls, bags of books, charts and tables, containing everything from Avicenna to al- Razi. All the knowledge of the world was there, though it seemed to me that al-Hakim was able to carry it complete in his own head.

At noon of the second of this hottest of summer days, we crested a dune to see a mirage of sails billowing on the shimmering horizon, but as we sallied nearer, would it solidify into the army's camp, grasping like near-drowned sailors unto the raft of an oasis. The biggest tent of all billowed up to a shining golden crescent. Here lay the great and fevered Saladin, whose urgent summons had bid us to mount our camels.

Our sultan had retreated to this forlorn place to lick his army's wounds, which were made more forlorn from defeat at the hands of the most successful of the infidels, Melech Ric. This monster is known to his countrymen as Richard, Coeur-de-Lion, and he is the king of a far-off little island named England. May Allah permit His Jjinns to forever curse this Richard's lion heart.

The perimeter guards knew my master well, and thus we were able to proceed directly to the great Saladin's tent. We swung down from our camels to approach a phalanx of the Sultan's proud mameluks, several of whom eyed me in a way more common to my former life. Dear Reader, I have grown, alas, accustomed to such looks. I smile and look down in modesty, for what Allah has bestowed must not be censured.

The sultan's tent was one of many lobes, a silken palace bedecked with hanging lamps and floored with Persian carpets of surpassing richness. A vizier said "Allah be praised," and led us to the deepest lobe, where lay the Greatest of the Great upon a mound of silken pillows.

My master *salaamed* and made a speech of worthy subjugation too flowery and long for my poor memory, which the sultan, in simple goodness, just waved aside saying, "Come, friend, and feel my brow, as you always do." This was offered in a voice of fevered strength, which made me kneel and cower in proper silence by the entrance. Al-Hakim then felt with reverence his master's brow, and pulse, and other parts.

"Describe, exalted one, your feelings."

"First there is the fever's heat. Did I tell you that one week ago Melech Ric was also struck down with a fever? Yet he roused himself from his bed and doomed my siege of Jaffa. My friend, you should have seen him, swinging his great axe before the city walls, cutting my best troops to shreds. I was so impressed, may Allah forgive me, that I sent him one of my best horses with the message that a king should only fight from the back of a great steed.

"Then there is an ache in my belly. Have I said that my scouts tell me that Richard has restored the battlements of Acre? And this, just after I had destroyed the walls of Ascalon in order to render them unfit for the defense of infidels.

"And my head throbs with a sharp pain. Did you know that I signed a secret treaty of allegiance with Conrad de Montferrat, which would have split the French army in two, and thus weakened Melech Ric's forces by a quarter?

"What cleverness, my Sultan," said my master.

"Yet two days ago...Oh my poor head...must I learn of Conrad's death. It was, of course, the work of the <u>Assassins</u>. And this morning, my spies tell me that Richard sent the enabling contribution to the killers' Sultan, The Old Man of the Mountain. Oh much-skilled friend of friends, rid me of this illness.

"My limbs ache too. How I envy your seeming youth, though you surpass me by a decade. Ah, but I am not as clever and good and as learned as my esteemed physician. Allah be praised for such friends."

This scene of two simple comrades, though both of transcendent greatness, did move me to silent tears. Then it was my master's turn to speak.

"Oh most high Sultan, might we play the Persian game?"

"Be gone physician, this is no time to joke. Melech Ric might at any moment discard his fever and move out to take back holy Jerusalem, and you suggest a game!"

"No, Oh Esteemed One, I suggest that a great game has caused the illness of both your exalted self as well as the King of Infidels. Many times, oh finest of friends, have you and I played chess."

"And many times has my physician played the fool and let me win."

"No. Never, Great One. No more than Richard. Think how you removed a castle and he removed a knight. Yet you have the advantage of many spies. Know you not his every move?"

"Of course, Friend of the Ages. I know the number of his troops and the direction of their movement within moments of his deciding. It is like playing chess with the opponent's game all written down. But then his spirit conquers, and inspires his men to win despite my well-laid traps. And thus are we ever at that worst of outcomes for the Persian game—mere stalemate. Oh how I long to put him in check. Thanks be to Allah that another fever lays him low. And now my agents tell me that Richard calls out in his misery for fruit and cooling drink. May all of Allah's Jjins parch his throat and burn his soul!"

"Aha!" said my Master, with a burst of glee that made both the Sultan and me jump with surprise. "You have pronounced the cure for your own illness and a checkmate for Richard!"

"I have? Then why call for you? Yet, al-Hakim, I must again pay your high fee for apparently only you can explain the cure that I have found."

"Oh Saladin, give me some peaches and snow and I will cure you."

I cowered the more, amazed that these two wondrous old men would use their simplest names for their exalted selves. And I had been allowed to witness this.

My physician worked through the night in a fine tent provided by his sultan. He did not mix potions, but summoned the sultan's spies, and after interviewing them for hours, wrote and wrote on parchments. I could not sleep and so, when morning rays of sun made our tent walls glow, was ready for his biding.

"Ahmad"—Ah, Dear Reader, did I not tell you my name?—"Ahmad, here is my first prescription. Take this letter and that bag of dinars to your former owner."

"But Master, what can Abad ibn-Aman have in the way of drugs that would cure our sultan?"

"We are not playing doctor for this cure, Ahmad. We are playing chess, and you are my first chess piece. Read it." I did, and shook my head in wonder, and left that morning for Jerusalem.

I can tell you now that others left as well. Some went north to fetch the very best pears and peaches. Two men were dispatched, using the fastest of horses, to visit mountain tops. Still others, skilled carpenters, did not leave but worked through night and day to form a cunning casket.

I returned, one day after, with the four companions that my master had requested. He took them into his tent.

"Remove your turbans and caftans." They did this, standing naked before him. Then did I more formally present my ingredients for his prescription.

"Here Master are your four chess peices. First Badir." Now stepped forth a Persian, the prettiest of boys, with fine transparent skin and long black hair that descended to his waist. "Second, Abu." He was a Nubian, with lithe muscles and a skin of deepest ebony, but unlike so many of his kind who shaved their heads completely, he preserved a top knot of hair that trailed down his back. "Third, Cheng Zee." A name—so you Dear Reader must have guessed—of oriental heritage. Stood he with golden winsome grace, and a long black braid. "And last, Bondel." He was the product of a union between a Frenchman and a Syrian concubine, and thus crowned his pale, well-sculpted body with a golden mane.

My master examined them, not in the way of any lasciviousness, but with all the dispassionate skill of his profession. Then he asked them, in French, of their skills of love, and was pleased when they answered in the same tongue.

"You have done well, Ahmad. I asked for all the races, for fine bodies, for long hair, for knowledge of French and for the secret skills. You have provided all, and now I have my knights and rooks. Much thanks."

The next morning a strange caravan left the sultan's camp, going west toward Jaffa. Twelve camels were employed. Al-Hakim rode the first. Next came five beasts bearing me as well as my four companions. Another carried a man whom I had never seen before, with hair and beard of an unworldly red color. Then four more camels, each carrying a pair of musicians, who strummed on lyres or blew on flutes during much of the journey. The last camel groaned and sputtered under a load of weird wooden frames. Our finale consisted of two handsome white horses that walked side by side bearing a yoke-like frame on which rested a large finely decorated casket. And on our flanks marched sixteen of the sultan's mameluks.

As the sun climbed toward noon, my master beckoned, and so I guided my camel to his side.

"Do you remember, Ahmad, our great sultan's reference to the Assasins?"

"Yes, Master."

"What do you know of them?"

"That they are a secret sect from the north sworn to kill anyone whom their own sultan, The Old Man of the Mountains, so directs, even if it is at their own peril."

"Yes. But do you know how this sultan inspires such fanatic loyalty?"

"No, Master."

"Ah that is a story of murderous deceit, caused by the sweetest of deceptions. When the Old Man's agents wander through the poorer villages of his domain, they are always on the lookout for young men and boys possessed of strength and bravery. And, finding one, they entertain him with strong drink and hashish. Hence the murderous name of the sect, which comes from Hashishin.

"When the chosen young man has been drugged into the point of insensibility, they take him to their sultan's secret valley, where, upon waking, the boy is told that here is Paradise. And behold, it is just as the All-Knowing Prophet said.

"Lush trees perfume the air with their fruits and flowers. Beautiful music comes from all directions. Succulent food and heady drinks are disported on every knoll. And the most exquisite ladies of the sultan's harem play the part of heavenly houris. The boy is showered with all the delights that can be imagined.

"That night his final banquet is drugged, and the next morning he awakes back in the impoverished village of his birth, whereupon his guides tell him that he has seen Paradise, whence he can return only through dying or doing his sultan's bidding."

"That is a wonderful story, Master, but how does it concern our present adventure?"

"Do you see those low hills to the west?"

"Yes, Master."

"Beyond lies Richard's camp. Now look to your left. There is another nest of rolling hills."

"I see them."

"Good, for the valley that they enclose will be the place where we shall make a Paradise. Our camels carry fruit and perfumed flowers to hang on all the trees. The musicians play as we speak. The banquet is in our camel bags. And you are one of the five houris."

"But who will be our guest?"

"Ah, we have reached that point where the others must journey to the valley, but you and I, and the two horses with their casket, will go west, to fetch the guest."

Here would my Master stop and give his instructions to the little army, in the form of copiously written parchments. Then the red bearded man got down from his camel and climbed through a secret panel in the bottom of the casket. And I grew curious indeed.

The heat of mid-afternoon bore down upon us as we topped the hills to see King Richard's camp. Al Hakim and I were on foot, leading the two horses with their yoked load.

"While you journeyed to Jerusalem, Ahmad, I mixed up some elixirs. We must drink one now," said he, taking a draught from a small blue-glass bottle. I full of trust, did also drink. "Now have we donned our armor against drugged peaches. Let us descend." A host of strange tents had been set up before the distant walls of Jaffa.

No sooner had we resumed the road, when two infidel knights stormed toward us on seeming steel horses that left great trails of dust. My master held out his hand in a signal to freeze—and I did so, trembling at the sight of a lance that was poised just before my chest.

"What brings you here, wretched pagans?" said the tallest of the armored giants, in a lingua franca that all have grown to understand since the infidels came to our land.

"We bear gifts from Mighty Saladin to King Richard," said my Master.

"Best beware of Greeks bearing gifts," said the other knight, in French, which I do understand quite well from the needs of my former profession. For Dear Reader, I must tell you that in the days of peace (Allah be praised) which followed our sultan's recapture of Jerusalem (Allah be twice praised), many Franks visited the house of Abad Ibn-Aman, and not a few wished to sleep with boys.

"Ah, but see and taste our fruits," said my master, opening the chest born by the horses. Here, on a bed of whitest, purest snow, where lustrous pears and peaches. He tossed a pear to each. They caught and sniffed them, and then, with slit-eyed looks at us, ate them. And after, licking his lips, the shorter one mercifully raised the lance that he had aimed at my heart.

"Come then, heathens, and we'll escort you to the king."

One rode ahead, and the other behind, with the reminder of his lance hovering at my back.

As we walked through the camp, many other men at arms came out to see us, though they seemed to me to look more like tin crustaceans. And I secretly laughed to see them shade their iron armor from the sun by wearing copies of my burnoose. So must all conquerors be conquered by their enemies. I was glad of our more sensible apparel.

Now came we to Richard's tent, as big as that of our sultan, yet so strangely shaped. Two long ungainly rectangular wings spread from its square center, and at the very top of this rigid construction was the hated cross of the infidels. Tents, think I, should be like a woman, with a round and graceful womb. Broad red and blue stripes ascended the sides of this ugly thing, the red was emblazoned with gold lions, and the blue with tiny gold flowers.

Melech Ric's own mameluks stood guard at his portal, yet were their faces hid by iron helmets. And then his vizier stepped forth to greet us.

"State your business, unbelievers," said this rough-hewn, untidy bearded man, who wore no armor.

"Oh great Vizier," said my master, with a strange movement that the Franks call a bow, "I am Abondek al-Hakim, personal physician to the Sultan of Sultans, Saladin. He sends me and my humble assistant, as well as these snow-cooled peaches," and here did my master reach back and reopen the casket, "as his gift to noble Richard of the Lion Heart, in hopes of aiding the recovery of a brave and glorious adversary."

Reader, have I not told you of my master's eloquence?

"I am Sir Thomas de Multon, Lord of Grisland and Count of Vaux," said the vizier. (And, Dear Reader, how I remembered all of that meaningless mumble shall remain a great mystery.) The vizier continued, "How, physician, are we to know if your sultan's gifts be honorable and untainted?"

"Oh revered Thomas de Multon, let me eat any peach of your choosing," said my master, "and my lowly helper will consume any pear."

Thomas chose and we ate. A minute or so later, when neither of us had seemed to faint or clutch our bellies with pain, would he relax and smile just a bit.

"Now might your grace of Multon ask his guardsmen to help us take this casket to the mighty Richard?" said my master with yet another bow.

His grace nodded and clapped, and four knights stepped forward to bear the casket to the King. We followed, and my Master winked at me.

The great chamber of the King's tent was furnished with strange, rigid furniture. Hard wooden chairs surrounded a dark ugly table, strewn with maps. Then we were ushered into a tapestry-draped bedchamber. "The lord of Grisland" gave a silent signal, and his four guardsmen put down the chest of fruit and withdrew. The three of us stood by the entrance curtains.

"Your most gracious and puissant Majesty," whispered Sir Thomas to a bundle under the covers of the biggest bed that I had ever seen. The bundle rumbled, yet remained covered. "Your Majesty, the Sultan Saladin has sent you gifts."

Now did the bundle erupt. Pillows flew away, covers dropped, and I watched in awe as a man with red hair and a red beard rose to sit up upon the silken sheets. I gave a wink of sudden understanding to al-Hakim, whose stern look waived me off.

"What gifts?" asked the fevered figure.

"He sends you pears and peaches and snow, my honored liege," said Sir Thomas, with a bow more florid than that of my master, "and the services of al-Hakim, who is the Sultan's personal physician."

"Search them," came his sovereign's answer. Sir Thomas turned to most impersonally (thanks be to Allah) run his hands over both of our bodies.

"Nothing, my King."

"Then bring me a peach," said Melech Ric, with a smile that defeated fever. Sir Tomas did so. "Oh wonderful! Another! And have one yourself, Thomas." He did.

Soon both men toppled into sudden sleep.

"Hurry Ahmed, stand by the drapes and watch the outer chamber," said my master as he rapped three times upon the base of the casket. A panel opened and the red headed man slithered out. "Quickly, quickly. We have only moments," whispered my master. Then he reached into the folds of his turban and pulled out a tiny vial of red glass, which he held to the lips of the King.

"Now," said al-Hakim to his red headed companion, "let us put him in the box." Whereupon did they set aside the tray of snow and peaches, pull back the rest of the covers to reveal a king's nakedness, and place him in the bottom of the casket. After they replaced the tray, the red-headed man stripped off his outer clothes, taking only his sharp dagger, and slipped beneath the covers of the bed.

"Good Gamal, seem to sleep deeply for one night, and tomorrow we will rescue you. Sweet dreams, my friend." Now the physician turned to me. "Help me raise poor Thomas of Grisland to this chair." I helped, and then my Master held a green vial under the knight's nose.

"Sir Thomas, awake, the heat has undone you!"

"Wh...what?" blurted the Englishman.

"A thousand pardons, honored Knight," said al-Hakim with yet another bow, "I was so busy attending to your exalted king that I did not notice that you shared his fever."

"No, no. I have felt quite well."

"Ah, perhaps it is the infernal heat, oh Count of Vaux. Still I would feel much better if you would humor an old physician by answering this one test." Here did al-Hakim take up a pendant, which hung from his own neck. "Follow with your eyes this ruby. See it sway. Left. Right. Up. Down. Yes, Sir Thomas, that is good. Yes, see it sway so calmly as you yourself are calmed. So very calm. Asleep while waking. Your king will also sleep deeply now, and wake tomorrow afternoon most wonderfully restored. You must let him sleep this sleep of cures. Do not for anything disturb him."

"But the heathens..."said Sir Thomas in a dreamy way.

"I tell you not to worry, Knight of Grisland, on my word of honor—May Allah strike me dead, if Saladin mounts an attack while your king sleeps. No oath comes higher than that which I have offered. Calm your fears. Oh so calm. Nothing but calm. And when I wake you, you must call for help to move the casket to our horses, for tomorrow we shall return with more delicacies."

"Yet these may serve to refresh others."

"Ah no, Sir Thomas, they were meant only for the king. We will return tomorrow with much, much more for all of you. Wake now Sir Thomas." My master whisked away the swaying amulet.

Sir Thomas stood up and clapped. The soldiers came. And we were— oh such thanks be to Allah—soon gone from King Richard's camp.

We trotted eastward bestride the horses, with our precious cargo strung between. I read, while riding, al-Hakim's last parchment, which detailed my role in "Paradise."

"Why Master, are all our houris males?"

"The spies gave me this final clue, Ahmad. Richard has never bedded with Berengaria, his new wife, nor any other woman, and has a deep loathing for his mother, Eleanor of Aquitaine. Not long ago he lusted for the king of France, then aged twenty. That is ten years his junior. And all of his youngest pages must spend sleepless nights.

"Mohammed tells us in his wisdom, that Hell holds nothing but that which a man hates. Yet Paradise abounds with all that he loveth."

"I understand all now, Master, and will play the role of your houri Queen."

"And I will be the hidden Chess King, the Old Man of the Shadows, and wait for you to elicit the magic words that will mean 'Checkmate'."

We rode up to the valley entrance. Four of our mameluks took charge of the horses and their precious cargo. Others stayed to guard the perimeter, as we went down into the valley.

From springs high in the hills, two clear and sparkling streams flowed nearly parallel to feed a glistening crystal lake, and on the grassy peninsula thus formed was set a fantastic pavilion. It's canopy, held up on golden poles and being of the sheerest silk, was transparent to the sky, even now in the throws of a brilliant sunset. No side drapes obscured the view of flowered trees and fruited shrubs. Eight Turkish lanterns hung above, and in the pavilion's center was a most remarkable construction, being a circular frame, strung with a web of twine and set on legs to form a waist-high platform. Beneath were all the "tools" that we would need.

"You have done well. Much thanks to you all," said my master to his band. "Ahmad, this frame is the last piece of the puzzle. It comes from the Sultan's workshops and is a loom designed for weaving carpets of a circular form. Now we shall snare our guest in its twine web." And as he spoke I could see the four mameluks take the sleeping naked Richard from the casket and tie his arms and legs, with softest fleece, so that his body might lie flat in an "X" upon the frame.

"Is all in readiness?" said my Master. "Then musicians play!" They did, like a cooing song of soft breezes. "Let the Houris take their positions." We did, our hair unbound, our caftans as translucent as the canopy, our places at some remove, facing away, like female statues in the near distance.

The sun had dipped below the encircling hills and stars began to peek through the silken canopy. The mameluks took up torches to ignite little hidden bonfires that would illuminate the fruited trees, and then retired from our sight.

"All is indeed ready." Then my master held the green vial beneath the nose of King Richard, and after, retreated behind the cover of a nearby flowered bush.

We all faced away, and thus could not see the expression on the king's face as consciousness returned, but soon we heard him. First a groan, then a growl as he shook at his bindings. Then a roar. "Arrrrh! Sir Thomas! Where are...Sir Guy and Sir Robert!...What in Hell's name is this?"

"Welcome," said I, turning and beginning to walk to him.

"Ah, no, I have been taken!" he shouted up to the canopy.

"Welcome," said Badir, also turning and slowly walking toward his right foot.

"The heathens have captured your king!" he screamed.

"Welcome," said Abu, walking inward to his left leg

"I will tell you nothing, pagan scum!"

"Welcome," said Cheng Zee, crossing to the right arm.

"Oh Jesus, Mary, and Joseph, save me now!"

"Welcome to Paradise," said Blondel, from the other side, "The prophet Jesus and his parents will come to you later, great king. In due time Moses and Mohammed and all of the other prophets will welcome you."

"Oh God help me!" he wailed, with the voice of a strangled child.

Now had we all reached the edge of the circle, saying in unison, "Allah welcomes you to Paradise." Then we let our caftans fall.

"Oh be damned you heathen creatures, think not that you can tempt a Christian King!"

"We are Allah's angels come to succor you, and welcome you to his Paradise," said Blondel.

"Begone, you devils. Angels have no penises or balls."

"Of course we do, for those who want that pleasure. Anything is possible in Paradise." Said Abu.

"No, by God's wounds, you are Moslem monsters bent upon a trick." He screamed, shaking with fury. "Why would your Allah welcome his greatest enemy to Paradise?"

"Because he loves your courage, great King," piped Badir with a sweet clear voice.

"Then know that I spit upon his people and his prophet." And he spat.

"Then know that Allah is ever merciful to heroes," said Cheng Zee.

"This is a trick. It is a trick. It is a trick!" screamed the King with eyes closed, thrashing against his restraints. "Why, you pagan shits, if this be 'Paradise,' am I then bound?"

"Because," said I, "those few unbelievers who are welcomed here must learn to trust, else they might do harm to others or themselves." I shot a look to my master's bush, and saw his hand rise in approval. "Now great King we will wash your body and cleanse you of all that is unworthy"

"Ah, now it comes. Scalding water to make me tell you all."

"No, great King, warmed water to soothe your body," said Cheng Zee, while we all dipped ocean sponges into bowls of the warm liquid, rich with fragrant soaps. He held himself rigid, as the four others washed inward from his hands and feet. I waited until they worked upon his head and torso, seeing his body relax despite all effort. Then did I run both soapy sponge and fingers about his privates. He stiffened again, and growled, then moaned and his hands spread rigid into the air.

"I know you for the devil's agents, and I will not yield," said he through his teeth. But his penis warmed and grew.

Then reached we all down to take up jeweled daggers.

"Ah now you show your true colors, and will flay me with your knives!" said Richard with steely bravery, but his penis began to shrink.

"No great King, but we will give your youth back," said Badir.

"Oh no, the horrid heathen truth at last...you will unman me!"

It could not be helped. We laughed at him, only to see beyond, a stern al-Hakim rise from his bush to hush us.

"No, no," said I, "We will only shave your body." We somehow subsumed our smiles. "But—Richard of the Lion Heart—you must be still, for even here in Paradise, skin can be cut and blood may flow."

Cheng Zee and Blondel shaved his chest and lower arms. Abu and Badir did his legs. And I waited, smiling sweetly at a lion who closed his eyes in fear. But when my shining knife-edge floated at the top of his pubic hair, the Lion's eyes grew wide.

"No, please, no."

"Ah yes, great King, even this. Be very still."

The others reached in to hold his arms and legs. He threw his head back and tensed his neck, and I began the soft downward scraping. And as I did so somehow he softened, sinking into his web with a long sigh. When I was done, I reached out to hold his organ and felt the warmth return. The others likewise caressed his arms and legs.

"You glow again with youth great King," said I, as he began to stiffen below.

"And now..." He murmured something oh-so-softly.

"We did not hear great King," said Cheng Zee.

"I suppose my head and beard are next."

"Why no, King Richard," said I, "Red hair is rare in Paradise. Besides, the Prophet himself did have a beard. Allah blesses them. But now we must dry you with softest lamb's fleece." We did that, and a smile crossed his face.

"And next we will burnish your glow even more," said I, thinking of the perfumed oil. But he snapped his head up with wild eyes and stiffened against the ropes.

"With whips. Oh yes, I know it now. You will lash my skin!"

"Is that your wish great King?"

"No, no, please no."

"I think it must be, and we will gratify it."

"No...yes...Oh God...I am lost!"

And then, standing round the circle, we whipped him with our long hair. Working in a circular wave, lashing his torso and loins, and laughing as we saw his growing tumescence. Saw the Lion Heart shudder with joy. Heard him moan and say: "Please no, oh please God, oh yes, oh God." And then saw him erupt across his own chest.

"Allah is pleased," said we all in unison, stroking our selves over the King's body, watching the fire glow in his eyes, pointing our organs out over him. "Allah is well pleased." Stoking faster, watching as he opened his mouth and begged with his eyes. "And we succor the great King." And then we shot in marvelous unison, and he, mouth open, thrashing, trembling, and trying to lick the air.

"Now, oh Richard of the Lion Heart," said I, "We will clean you with our tongues and lips." Which, of course, we did while he writhed in—yes, Dear reader, it was joy. "And now the perfumed oil to add to your glow of youth." We reached down below the frame to bring up glass vials, and uncorked them.

"Allah has scented this oil with myrrh," said Badir, as he poured it on the King's left thigh.

"Allah has perfumed this with frankincense," said Abu, tipping his vial over the rigid stomach.

"Allah sends you rose-oil," said Cheng Zee, oiling the left tit.

"Allah has distilled the finest ambergris," said Blondel, pouring in the well of his collarbone. They spread and stroked and kneaded, over and down and under and around to those special places that al-Hakim had requested.

King Richard lost all thoughts of kingliness. His eyes glazed. His breath came in staccato bursts. His heart thumped audibly. And his penis throbbed with stiffness. It was my turn.

"And Allah, all praise to mighty Allah, Allah gives you the musk oil of the mountain beaver, for your most special needs." Oh Dear Reader, it was all I could do to stifle laughter for I knew this to be the oil of olives, augmented by an infusion of cloves and cinnamon. But I poured it on the tip of his straining organ. Let it drip down to his balls, and watched him twitch upon the web. Saw his hips bucking with need. Witnessed his rigid penis stab upward into the air. Then ever so lightly ran my finger along the lips of the glans and down the soft bottom ridge of the shaft, while the others kneaded every bit of him, and sang a soft song of Allah's praise.

But then I saw the sign of his imminent eruption, and as per my master's instructions, withdrew and gave the signal for the others to stop. Richard bucked wildly, and now, eyes wider than ever, realized that we had abandoned him.

"Oh no, don't stop, oh for the love of G...no, for the love of Allah...no, no...Oh Jesu... please, no, I need...Oh Allah, please!"

My master was no longer hidden. He stood frozen with interest by the bush. And signaled us to continue. Cheng Zee and Blondel stepped forward to place their erect organs within reach of Richard's hands. Badir and Abu used theirs to nuzzle his feet. And while his fingers and toes grasped and fondled, the four houris undid his bonds, saying "Allah releases you, great King, and our bodies are his gifts to you for pleasure in his Paradise."

But he did not try to escape. Instead the king stretched out his feet to continue fondling, as best toes could, the organs of Badir and Abu. And his hands would not relax their greedy grasp of Blondel and Cheng-zee. So now must I begin my climactic role by climbing up upon the frame and then descending to sit on Richard's so-stiff penis. I took him inside of me with every trick that I had learned, my hands held back upon his knees, my legs thrust forward, toes pointed to go under his arms, then up, to massage his neck and cheeks, while my nether region sucked, and thrust, and slithered upon his manhood. And Reader, he succumbed—he trembled in ecstasy, screaming—

"Oh yes, oh wonderful, oh G...NO! oh Allah, oh Great Allah!" Then did he shoot forth within me, screaming "Allah, Allah, Allahoo Akbar!" We all ejaculated, covering him with strings of burning pearls, and still he said, over and over, the name of the one true God.

I looked aside to see my master, dancing with glee beside his bush. He gave me the sign of finger drawn across the throat—which I knew to be, Dear Reader, not a signal for assassination, but feasting. So all of us climbed upon the loom. Licked at the king's trembling body. Snuggled and cooed into his writhing arms and legs. And reached down for treats of fruit and drink.

"A candied fig for you my King."

"Sweet grapes all peeled for your lips."

"A pomegranate, dipped in honey."

"Some fine wine from your province of Anjou."

"And luscious peaches, snow cooled for a king."

He tasted all, and all were drugged.

Al Hakim came forward to hold his red vial to sleeping Melech Ric's lips. Then the mameluks placed him in the bottom of the casket. New delicacies, undrugged of course, were now brought forth, and we did feast—five Houris, al-Hakim, and all of the mameluks, on figs and honey, on peaches and each other, throughout the wee hours of the night.

A pink and silver dawn discovered me, my master and the two white horses standing on the crest above King Richard's camp. He, of course, was sleeping beneath a tray of undrugged banquet pleasures. The two sentry knights galloped forth again, and with a bribe of honeyed pomegranates, led us to that ugliest of tents.

Sir Thomas greeted us, called forth four knights to take up the casket, and ushered us in to the bedchamber. Then, with a clap, he excused the knights.

"The king sleeps soundly as you said he would." And here did the lord of Grisland indicate a knotted bundle in the middle of the great bed.

"And you, Great Lord?" said al-Hakim.

"Oh well, indeed."

"Permit me once again," said my master, swaying his ruby amulet.

Sir Thomas slipped into a trance and simply stood there, watching all with a smile of sweet dreams, as two red headed men were exchanged. Then my master snapped his fingers.

"You see, physician, I am fit again," said the Lord of Vaux, with a smile.

"Indeed. Now let us see to the King." Whereupon did al-Hakim hold the green vial under Richard's nose.

"Allah...All...A..." The King clutched the covers to his chest and stared, wide-eyed, around the room, and screamed. "Sir Thomas, call the guards, I have been taken!"

"No my liege, you are here, quite safe, in your own bedchamber."

Then the king's eyes lit on me.

"Him. I know those eyes. Take off his burnoose!"

Sir Thomas did so, revealing my bald head. Oh Reader—I was not happy when a shaving proved to be the banquet's finale—yet now I understood. King Richard looked away and cowered 'neath his covers.

"Tis naught but a dream caused by the fever," said my master, "More sleep will see him rise in splendor. Now, Sir Thomas, could you help us to take these fruits to that tray, for my sultan has asked that his casket be returned."

"No, take them back," screamed the king from his damask bundle, "I would fain never see such fruits again. Out! Away with all of you!"

"But..." Sir Thomas reached quickly for a peach, as my master closed the lid. Then with a sigh, he clapped his hands. The four knights returned, and I once again thanked Allah as we rode from Richard's camp.

"*Shoukran* Ahmad. My thanks to all, and most of all to Allah. Thus checkmate for Melech Ric and a cure for Saladin. We have just assassinated the spirit of a Christian king."

And, indeed, within two weeks would Richard of the Lion Heart sign a treaty of peace and then sail away. Never—Thanks be to Allah—to return.

But you, Dear reader, may not see fit to thank Allah, for I must close with more poesy—

Fear not the infidel's battle axe,
Nor his steel case from neck to shin.
Lamb's fleece hath doomed the Lion's heart,
And soft gold Arab skin.

Will's Best Bed

"Item: I gyve vnto my wife my second best bed with the furniture."
This hastily scrawled afterthought may be read
near the end of Shakespeare's will.

London in the days of Good Queen Bess was a city surrounded by suburbs with names that might have served as titles for bawdy poems: Pamlico and Black Heath, Clerkenwell and Newton Butts, Spittalfields—and the one where Will Shakespeare chose to live—Shoreditch. One imagines a ballad wherein drunken sailors and their doxies wallow amidst the muddy ruts, yet the name was a half-truth, for though ditches were legion, the nearest shore was miles away.

The ditches ran thick with muck. Wine dregs from the taverns mixed with offal from the butcheries and fish stalls, to say nothing of the odorous soup of horse, dog and sheep dung that stewed in ruts by every road. And over all hung the sick-sweet smell of human waste, especially when slops buckets were emptied from upper windows belonging to countless houses of dubious repute.

One truly sweet thing might shimmer through the air of Shoreditch, and that was when the bells of St.Leonard's called the too-few faithful to worship. Otherwise the local sounds seemed as raucous as the smells were rank. Street vendors squawked out their wares. Drovers harangued their herds on the way to slaughter. Wagon wheels rumbled and horses whinnied under the crack of whips. On many afternoons a clangor of trumpets and drums announced performances at the playhouses. This was one reason why, despite the noisesome atmosphere, Shakespeare had chosen Shoreditch as his place of residence. Both The Curtain and The Theatre were within a minute's walk. Many other players and playwrights agreed. Christopher Marlowe lived around the corner in a cul-de-sac called Norton Fulgate.

Will lodged above a greengrocer's shop on Shoreditch High Street. Visitors had to brave the muddy ruts, open the street door, and either turn left to haggle over barrels and crates of vegetables, or scurry right to a ramshackle stairs that crooked its way up to a rudely paneled door. Here might be found the budding playwright of the age. His two rooms were large enough, yet their renter being of a parsimonious nature, bare and simple in the outfitting. At front, the anti-chamber served as parlor, study, dining room, and due to the presence of the only fireplace, kitchen. The meager furnishings included a small trestle table, two benches, the tiniest of hutches, and one Windsor chair.

At the rear, to the side of the fireplace, would be found the door to the chamber, a room every bit as commodious, but even meaner in its décor. A joint-stool and the slops bucket sat by the back window. Two trunks huddled along a side wall; one for clothes and the other for books. Will's well-locked money box was hidden under those books. And just to the left, backed up to the chimney bricks for warmth of a winter's night, was a bed that no man could call best.

Four raw wood staves formed a narrow rectangle held up by stubby, rough-cut legs. A net of rope stretched across the frame to serve as springs. The mattress was a bag of canvas stuffed with straw; the sheet, an un-hemmed square of homespun. Will's one touch of luxury was a linen pillow filled with goose down. In short, a bed that served for fits of sleep, but nothing else.

Not that there had been anything else. Four years ago Master Shakespeare had left a wife and three offspring behind in Stratford-Upon-Avon. One mustn't say abandoned. He continued to send a portion of his earnings back for their sustenance. And the earnings had been growing, not only the wages of a hired man in the company of Lord Pembroke's Men, but also remunerations from three successful plays provided for the company's repertory. At the age of twenty-nine, William Shakespeare was becoming a name to conjure with those of Christopher Marlow and Thomas Kyd.

Why had he left Anne and the children? Not because his wife was disagreeable or the children unpleasant. Though it was sad that she had not enough learning to read his poems, nor the children sufficient manners to be quiet and let them happen. Perhaps because he had found that being a lawyer's clerk had trapped all language in a cage of writs. How tempting it had been when the players came to Stratford, and Will heard that their company was short an actor or two. No grand future was promised, but still, to join a group of men and boys whose dearest passion was the recitation of fine words...ah that was a wondrous prospect! It was a temptation not to be resisted. And perhaps—something Will realized only of late—perhaps because a place like Shoreditch, being outside of the city's walls and therefore beyond its laws, was known as one of the London 'Liberties'.

But liberty for what? For something to do with the company of men and boys. For something tantalizingly beyond the realm of present poesy. For...for the newly realized beauty of neither men nor boys, but for the in-between. No, farther along than that. For that time of youth just beyond the verge of manhood. Beyond the piping voice of boyhood for which, in future, Will would write a Desdemona or a Juliet, and beyond the throaty croaking for whom a Viola or Rosalind might be created. But just beyond. That lovely time when a young man's voice sounded with the clarity of a trumpet, when cheek fuzz strove toward stubble, when soft smooth skin began to know the sinews underneath, and when innocence trembled on the edge of...a sensual incipience.

> Oh fleeting time of beauty's fine first fling.
> Oh lovely days of budding manhood's Spring...

No, no, it would not do. Will crumpled the paper and threw it into the slops bucket. He had often watched such youths, usually between the ages of seventeen and twenty. They were once the ones who had once played female parts, bowing at play's end, laughing as they skipped off to the tiring house, then tearing off their dresses, pulling pins to let their hair fall, daubing away the painted cheeks and lips, and standing for a moment nude, smiling at the looking glass. But now, playing roles more Romeoesque, they strutted by the mirror.

Yet never would Will sully his reputation for probity by cavorting with company youths. Let Marlowe chase the playhouse boys and carouse in taverns and dice his life away. Master Shakespeare aspired to be accepted as a gentleman. That was not easy to do in the summer of 1592. Plague once again besieged London.

The playhouses were closed, and touring had proved such a disaster that the company had dispersed for the summer. Money was tight. Will tried his hand at poetry of a different stripe, hoping for the rewards of lordly patronage. A long and lyrical ballad entitled *Venus and Adonis* struggled to take shape upon his writing table. Oh, did he dream of youthful Adonis, and Venus's voice was Will's.

> "I'll be a park, and thou shalt be my deer;
> Feed where thou wilt, on mountain or in dale;
> Graze on my lips; and if those hills be dry,
> Stray lower, where the pleasant fountains lie."

He was but a third or so on the way to completion. And to whom might he apply for the all important patronage? My Lord Pembroke? Or better the Earl of...But then insistent knocks sounded from the door. Will opened it to see a tall gaunt fellow, stiff, long-nosed, and looking down it.

'Art Master William Shakespeare?'

'I am.'

'My Lady, the Countess of Southampton, requires audience of you.'

'Pray when?'

'Pray now, and at her rooms, and quite Post Haste. You are, in short, to come with me.'

'And to what purpose?'

'An commission, think I.'

'Well then, allow me to fetch my cap and cloak, and I will follow. Enter, sir.'

The emissary looked within.

'I think not," he sniffed, 'and shall wait below.'

The Countess's man strode rapidly ahead and said nothing. A long trek north of London's walls led past Finsbury Fields and on through Clerkenwell to find, in a place called Bloomsbury, a most handsome mansion. It was a towering house built in the latest Italianate taste. The factotum rang a bell at the gates and a porter swung them wide. Will followed across a fountained courtyard and up stone steps to arched doors worthy of a cathedral. This time the tongue of a bronze lion clutched a knocker ring, which the emissary raised, and with a sneer at Will, let fall with endless reverberations. One door creaked open and they walked into a Great Hall that might well have rivaled the nave of St. Paul's.

'That bench,' sniffed the long nose.

Will sat, staring up at soaring vaulting.

'I shall inform Her Grace of your attendance.'

Then the tall man hurried up a marbled staircase.

'Master Shakespeare, welcome to Southampton House. How good of you to come,' said the Countess, most musically, as she perched by a high balcony rail. Her voice echoed from the stonework. Will stood, and executed his most obsequious bow. 'Come, come up,' said she, 'the hall is too cold a place. We must needs meet in my cabinet.' She beckoned with imperious certainty. He hurried, then thought better of it, and paraded up the stairs in proper solemnity.

She led him to her antechamber, a vast room that darkly shined with polished oak and Flemish tapestries, and on through the chamber dominated by a bed that seemed a palace in itself. Ornate gilded columns held aloft a canopy which grazed the painted heavens of the ceiling. The countess crossed to the far wall and pressed upon a linenfold paneling of the high wainscoting, and then a door opened to her cabinet.

This was the most unexpected of honors. A common citizen might linger for a moment in the hall of such a house. More important folk would parley in an antechamber. Friends of comparable rank could trade confidences in the chamber. But only a truly exalted few ever ventured into the holy precinct of a noble's cabinet.

'Sit there, Master Shakespeare, upon that stool.'

He sat upon a hassock of gold carving and red velour worth the yearly wages of five ordinary citizens, set by a tortoise shell inlaid table centered in the cage of a towering oriel window that looked out upon manicured topiary gardens. She stood by a marble fireplace, resplendent in a gown of deep green taffeta upon which had been spun a web of pearls. And her age? Perhaps forty, but who could tell, painted as she was with a porcelain mask of white lead oxide. The lady gestured towards a painting hanging by the fireplace.

'Surely thou knowest my son, Henry, Earl of Southampton.'

'Yes My Lady, he comes often to watch us play, and though I've not met with him, still, his presence hath been pointed out.' Answered Will, who had many times peeked beyond the arras curtain to spy the elegant young gentleman, so beautiful as he lounged at the Lord's Room railing of the lower gallery.

'Yes, too often,' said the Countess with an icy smile, 'He doth love only plays and poesy, as well as gaming and hunting and fine apparel. We needs must coax him to another love, and that is why thou hast been summoned.'

'Another love?'

'Yes, one more proper and, to the point, advantageous. This love.' Then the Countess handed Will a miniature portrait in a casing of gold and jewels. The subject was a young lady coiffed and costumed as grandly as the queen. 'Master Hilliard has done his best to paint her most attractive features, but my son will only fondle the frame.'

'And my part, Your Ladyship?'

'To woo him to her. To paint with words a picture even more alluring.'

'And the lady?'

'She is the granddaughter of Lord Burley, affianced by careful contract to my son some four years past. Henry was fifteen years of age then and she but twelve. He hath delayed and dodged for four long summers, and now refuses to give her his hand. Imagine, a union between two of England's greatest families as well as fortunes. To say nothing of the necessity for an heir.'

'And you have told him this?'

'Too many Ands, poet. I have cooed, cajoled, cried, and called out a cacophony of reasons. Have pleased and pleaded, and even prostrated my self before him. Lord Burley has likewise reasoned, remonstrated, and even threatened recourse to the law. Henry will hear none of it, in fact, will hear nothing of any marriage at all.'

'But what words would you have of me?'

'Why poems, poet. Smooth words to woo a young man into sense. Are not sonnets the fashion? Thou shalt write honeyed songs of love.'

'But...'

'Too many Buts as well.. Ten sonnets for ten Pounds, and by Friday next. My man will visit you with Pounds in hand. See to it that he returns with poems.'

'And...'

'And it is time to say good day to you, Master Shakespeare. Write fast and well.'

And so would be born the first of the famous Sonnets. Will began by diving into his library trunk, then visiting booksellers, reading other poets' sonnets to find, not the form for that was easy, but the fashion. Many were paeans to a lady's beauty, which, from the earl's dismissal of the miniature, offered little prospect of success. Others dwelt on yearnings for a loving union, but this too was an argument that must prove fruitless. And some sang of the pain caused by separation, yet the young man obviously gloried in his distance and disdain.

What to do, what to write? Will had dithered for four days and Friday loomed. If only the commission could had been reversed. How happy he would have been to woo the young lady by praising the beauty of the youthful earl...so happy, as well as inspired.

Here was a portrait already engraved upon Will consciousness. Not only had he watched Southampton through the arras. He had several times, while acting, forgotten his words—and in his own plays—when his eyes strayed past the other actors to spy the Adonis leaning on the Lord's Room rail. Such long golden hair spilling down over his lace ruff. Those luminous eyes that burned with sapphire blue. Features carved so delicate yet strong. Cheeks that glowed with warmth beyond the need for rouge. And his form: firm yet slender legs straining at the netherstocks, torso filling out the doublet, and fine grace in every stance. Perfection. Such a fleeting wonder was this Spring of manhood. Such a waste to age beyond the moment without leaving offspring as an heir to Spring. But wait, therein might be found a theme! Woo not the earl to the lady—woo the youth to fatherhood, thereby bequeathing to the world a shining simulacrum of his own radiance.

Thus were ten sonnets written in two days. Each worshiped a different aspect of Southampton's beauty. Each also warned of the ravages of time.

And each ended with the zing of a procreative couplet. The last sonnet's final couplet went further, perhaps too far.

> "Make thee another self for love of me,
> That beauty still may live in thine or thee."

Will almost scratched out that "for love of me," but left it, praying that, though those words were his truest hope, they might be read as coming from the Countess.

———————

Friday, and the bells of St. Leonard's were tolling the hour of noon when the insistent knocks sounded.

'Master Shakespeare,' sniffed the Countess's man, 'hast ten poems?'

'I do, and thou ten Pounds?'

'I do, but first must read the first.'

'First?'

'Sonnet, Sir.'

Will handed it over. His visitor's long nose twitched as he read.

'Most clever, Sir. 'Tis an argument not thought of by My Lady or Lord Burley. And the others follow in this line?'

'They do.'

'Then these ten Pounds are thine.' He set a bag of coins upon the table, took up the ribbon-tied roll of sonnets. 'Tomorrow the Earl returns from hunting at Titchfield. My Lady will have strewn these sonnets about His Lordship's chambers.' And he marched to the door. 'Ah yes,' he turned back, 'The Countess will have ten more such sonnets, and thus shall I return one week hence with ten more Pounds. And so adieu.'

Will wrote, and as his quill flashed across the page, the new sonnets underwent an unforeseen change. The eleventh followed the pattern of poetic nagging, ending with the thought that Nature had...

> "...carved thee for her seal, and meant thereby
> Thou shouldst print more, not let that copy die."

But the twelfth and fourteenth identified the writer with 'I's too masculine to be taken for a Countess, and showed him anxiously consulting the clock and then the stars. The next sonnet dropped hints that the writer might be an actor; the seventeenth that he was a poet. And the eighteenth threw aside all caution, to say nothing of nagging, and sang of love in a way that the future would consider to be classic.

> "Shall I compare thee to a summer's day?
> Thou art more lovely and more temperate."

And the twentieth more than hinted at just what kind of love.

> "A woman's face, with Nature's own hand painted,
> Hast thou, the Master Mistress of my passion;
> A woman's gentle heart, but not acquainted
> With a shifting charge, as is false woman's fashion.
> An eye more bright than theirs, less false in rolling,
> Guiding the object whereupon it gazeth;
> A man in hue all hues in his controlling,
> Which steals men's eyes and women's souls amazeth.
> And for a woman wert thou first created;
> Till Nature, as she wrought thee, fell a-doting,
> And by addition me of thee defeated
> By adding one thing to my purpose nothing.
> But since she pricked thee out for women's pleasure,
> Mine be thy love, and thy love's use their treasure."

'Oh God,' thought Will, lying upon his cramped little bed, still staring at those words. 'I have gone past the bounds.' He wanted to burn the sonnet, but could not bring himself to do it. He stared on and on, until sleep claimed him and brought forth lovely dreams.

The bells of St. Leonard's again sounded their carillon of noon, and once more were followed by insistent knocks. But this time the Countess's man was not alone. A tall figure, his face shrouded in a dark hooked cape, stood behind on the shadowed stairs. Will was suddenly wary, and very glad that he had put aside the last three sonnets.

'Hast ten more, Master Shakespeare?'

'Alas, no, my muse abandons me. There are only seven.'

'A disappointment to be sure, for both My Lady and her son.'

'None-the-less, there are but seven.'

'Then I must count out seven pounds, no more.' The which did he, and Will handed over the roll of sonnets.

'I have heard enough, Thomas, and you will wait for me below,' said the hooded one, taking the sonnets for himself.

'But...'

'Below...and while I think on it, wait not. I shall upbraid the recalcitrant poet and return in mine own good time.'

'Bu...'

'Go!''

The Countess's man hurried down the stairs. The hooded man stepped past a nervous Will and into the center of the chamber. He stood there, facing away, holding the roll in one hand and repeatedly slapping it into the other.

'I'll have the last three by tomorrow, an' it please you, Sir,' said Will with a catch in his throat.

The dark specter started to laugh, then turned and threw back his cloak to reveal a golden mane and two shining sapphire eyes, and thus did Master William Shakespeare meet Henry Wriothesley, Third Earl of Southampton. Will bowed his deepest bow.

'Thou art more fair in thy person, Master Shakespeare, than upon the stage.'

'My Lord, this is much praise from one as youthful and fair as thee.'

'I am nineteen years of age, and yourself?'

'Almost a decade more.'

'That decade hath not robbed thee of good looks, yet your sonnets say that I am soon to wither and lose mine own.'

'No, never that, mere poesy composed to meet thy mother's purpose.'

'Aye, and at a Pound per poem. Thus might a tiny ounce of ink grow to a pound of silver, and poesy become most weighty matter. Well done, Master Poet.'

'I would most happily have writ sans fee, My Lord.'

'No, no,' said the Earl, as he looked around the room, 'thou livest like a monk, and thy cell doth seem too plain a place for the conjuring of fine words. Such hard and simple benches, Will Shakespeare. Use thy pounds for comfort, and buy a cushion or two.'

Whereupon did the Earl seat himself in Will's one chair.

'When, five days past, did I return from Titchfield, I found myself at swim in a sea of sonnets. They were pinned to the bed curtain, placed 'pon my pillow and between the sheets, rolled up in one of my best boots, tacked to my closet door, papered to my mirror, even laid across the cover of my close stool. Art in luck that I had not wiped my arse with one.

'Yet when I read of them, here was a mirror that I grew to like, for I did see beyond the frame of my mother's carping, and looked intently to find deep within the silvered surface a loving image. And was both flattered and honoured to know that the mirror had been cast by such as thee. So seat thyself, Will Shakespeare, on one of thy hard, uncushioned benches, whilst I do read these others.'

Will sat, all the while gazing in wonder at this radiant apparition of his dreams.

'No wonder thy muse has fled, Master Shakespeare,' said Henry, as he finished reading the last sonnet, 'for she must tire of a tiresome theme. Would that thou had indeed writ sans fee, and therefore freely, for then thy mirror, unclouded by maternal dictates, might have reflected with more truth.'

Will abandoned caution, rushed back to his chamber, and returned with the withheld sonnets. 'Then here, My Lord, be thy true reflections.'

Henry Wriothesley sparkled into a radiant smile as he removed the ribbon, and began to read, mouthing the words "Shall I compare thee..." then fell silent as he devoured them. When he finished the twin sapphires burned even deeper blue as they looked up from the page, and Will ruby-blushed.

'That mirror, Will, be steamed with lovely passion, and I would hear thy voice recite the next.'

Will took the page. His voice started with a quaver, but warmed to an actor's threnody.

> "Devouring Time, blunt thou the lion's paws,
> And make the earth devour her own sweet brood;
> Pluck the keen teeth from the fierce tiger's jaws,
> And burn the long-lived phoenix in her blood."

'What, time again?' said his audience, 'Hast abandoned love so soon?'

> "Make glad and sorry seasons as thou fleet'st,
> And do whate'er thou wilt, swift-footed Time,
> To the wide world and her fading sweets;
> But I forbid thee one most heinous crime:"

'And I forbid thee, Will, to dwell again on Time!'

> "Oh carve not with thy hours my love's fair brow,
> Nor draw no lines there with thine antique pen;
> Him in thy course untainted do allow
> For beauty's pattern to succeeding men.
> Yet do thy worst Old Time. Despite thy wrong,
> My love shall in my verse ever live young."

'Ah good, thou hast, for love of me, delivered Time a killing blow.' Henry took up the last page. 'Now 'tis my turn to recite.' But he fell silent upon speaking "Master-mistress." Will froze in hopeful terror as Henry scanned the rest. He put the page down with a sigh.

'Th'art wrong, Will...

> Nature hath not pricked me out for women's pleasure,
> Mine be <u>thy</u> love, and my love's use <u>thy</u> treasure.
> And for these beauteous poems of wanton bliss,
> I'll pay thee not with pounds, but with a kiss.'

Oh such a kiss ensued. Lips grazed, tongues dueled, and hands so happily deflowered doublets. Next shirts were shed, and two pair of eyes devoured torsos.

Henry's eyes strayed lower.

'Thy codpiece straineth, Will. Wil't have release?'

'Thy will doth also show the same increase.'

'Ah, let's to bed, before our wills surcease.'

'Thy last rhyme is lumpin, as is my bed.'

'But willy-nilly, 'tis where thou shalt be led.'

Henry took Will's hand and opened the chamber door.

'But where...?'

'There, My Lord, I tried to tell...'

'That...rack! 'Tis naught but a bed for bruises.'

'It serves for sleep.'

'I see not how. Perhaps a poet needeth pain to poetise."

He marched back to the chamber and began dressing.

'And no carpets anywhere, just rough wood floors. Oh Will, love doth demand a bed of roses, or some soft comfort at the very least. Spend thou thy pounds for comfort, else I shall not love thee. But where else might we...? My Lady Mother would bar the gates of Southampton House, and Titchfield Hall is a long day's journey'.

He stood at the door, assuming his cloak and hood.

'Well, Will, we have a nest to seek. 'Til then adieu.'

Henry left, and Will staggered to the window to watch love's hooded form disappear amidst the noise and bustle of Shoreditch High Street.

Will spent the next week writing. He tried to finish *Venus and Adonis*, but no words would come. Besides, what hope had he now of an earl's patronage? He took long walks, searching for words, and too often ended up gazing past the gates of a certain grand house in Bloomsbury. And every day he wrote sonnets, sometimes more than one. More to the fashion too, for though the pronouns were He and I, they lamented lost love. One stands out for its central image.

> "Weary with toil, I haste me to my bed.
> This hard repose for limbs with travel tired;
> But then begins a journey in my head
> To work my mind when body's work expired;
> For then my thoughts, far from where I abide,
> Intend a zealous pilgrimage to thee,
> And keep my drooping eyelids open wide,
> Looking at darkness which the blind do see;
> Save that my soul's imaginary sight
> Presents thy shadow to my sightless view,
> Which, like a jewel in the ghastly night,
> Makes black night beauteous and her old face new.
> Lo, thus, by day my limbs, by night my mind,

For thee, and for myself, no quiet find."

Such sleepless nights on that rude bed, and then another Friday, and St. Leonard's bells.

When heavy knocks were heard, Will leapt towards his door, only to be disappointed when he found a short and burly workman standing on the stairs.

'Master William Shakespeare?'

'I am he.'

'Then I've a trifle to deliver to ye.'

Will held out his hand.

'No, no, 'tis a slightly larger trifle. Wait.' The man whistled back down the stairs, and four others tromped up bearing long beams carved with fancy moldings.

'Where be thy chamber, Master Shakespeare?' asked their leader.

'Why through that far door.'

The four stomped through and dropped their burdens, then tromped back down. Will wondered if these pieces were the frame for some large picture. Two returned lugging carved oak columns. Two others carried a tall paneled piece that bore a carving of Venus and Adonis...and Will began to understand.

Then all struggled, cursing, up the steps, groaning, heaving, and calling to the grocer's shop for more help. Will was right. A huge and wonderful bed was being delivered. He had not been forsaken.

The base was deep, thick, wide, and even tipped sideways, jammed in the doorway. But much pushing and more profanity finally succeeded forcing an entrance. One more trip brought up the curtains and other furnishings. The five men then began shoving and hammering and shouting as they assembled it. And the bed almost didn't fit, so tall was it that the cornice scraped the ceiling. They had to whittle down the pillar tops. It was night when they had finished, and every one of Will's few candles was burning.

He dipped into a wilting store of coin to give each man a parting gratuity.

'I'm to say that thou'lt be visited tomorrow by the giver of this gift,' winked the leader when he left. Will closed the door and retired to his chamber. Good God it was huge. Russet curtains trimmed with gold fringe soared up on three sides. The carved panel was the headboard. So like a stage! And such lovely furnishings within: Four silk pillows, velvet seeming blankets, and sheets of ivory linen. Oh such a bed...truly the very best of beds.

He could not wait until tomorrow. Forget supper. And Will was so full of happy anticipation that he doubted sleep was possible, even on such a wondrous bed. None-the-less, he undid the many knots of his doublet and hose, slithered out of them, and assumed his night gown. Will closed the chamber window, then went out to the antechamber, bolted the door, closed the front windows, and bent to blow out the candles on the trestle table, when he heard the piping of a recorder. And it came from the chamber!

He raced back to find that a sheet of parchment had been pinned to the closed curtains of the bed. Then the music stopped, and Will crept closer to read the message.

> For sweet and soothing sleep hath beds been made,
> Unless between the sheets there lies a maid,
> Or better yet the cambric cushion's plumped
> By fair Priapus hoping to be trumped.
> Thus do I play your willing master-maid,
> Unclothed, this bed my only masquerade.
> Oh Will, spread now these russet curtains wide.
> Spread me as well, then rush to plunge inside.

Oh did Will laugh as he spread the curtains. Henry, as naked as his word, did too.

'But how did you...?'

'I was delivered with the bed, Will, or rather in it.'

'No wonder it was so...'

'Heavy? And damned uncomfortable. I've more bruises about me now than if we had used thine old claptrap of a cot.'

'But in...'

'Yes, inside! Cunning is it not? There is a sliding panel 'neath the mattress. Twas my Father's, built years past for I know not what nefarious purpose. Oh, but you should have seen how Thomas and I had to scheme to get it down from a store room and thence carried here. My Lady Mother believes that I have taken it to Titchfield. But now tis here and yours...and so am I!'

Henry stood upon the bed, and grasped the collar of Will's night shirt.

'Away with this tent, for I would see thy pole.'
`He snatched it up and away.
'And thou dost not disappoint. Come, Will, to thy bed.'
Will leapt upon the bed, and descended into Henry's arms.

The next morning they awoke, most appropriately, with cocks crowing.

'What think thou, Will, of the poem?'
'The one that I did read, or the one I see beside me?'
'Both.'
'That which I read must, alas, be burnt.'
'Burnt? Twas that bad?'
'No, twas Heaven itself, but those words discovered would have us burnt, or rather, me. Buggery's a burning offence. Best not write words too plain. That may be half the art of poesy, suggesting without saying.'
'But if one only said, not writ, but said...'
'And the walls be thick, then safe.'
'Then burn it, but only if thou wilt say me now another sonnet.'
'Extempore?'
'Yes.'
Will kissed him, then rose and stood at the end of the bed. Stood like a naked actor.

The stage on which I most do love to play
Be not the Curtain, nor the newer Rose.
'Tis where I act by night instead of day,
In wanton joy, sans actor's gaudy clothes.
This playhouse hath a thatch of lustrous gold,
To shade the heaven of a star-gilt face.
A lean façade, fine sculpt in classic mould,
Displays an arras fringed with golden lace.
And there below thrusts out that sinew'd stage,
'Pon which I play with all my player's art,
To coax the love of youth despite my age,
And taste the pulsings of a noble heart.
Then grovel I, a groundling in the pit,

Exalting beauty that eclipses wit.

It was, like many such affairs, short lived. More sonnets would be written lamenting ever longer absences. Eventually Southampton would marry, but not Lord Burley's granddaughter. And many years later, when Will left London and came back to live a prosperous retirement in Stratford, the bed came with him.

Death came too, and the reading of the will. Anne sat stone faced as it was read. Most of Will's considerable fortune was left to his daughter, Susanna. Anne received only the aforementioned "item".

And the best bed? Will's lawyer announced that it had been, at the orders of Master Shakespeare, sold. Indeed the bill of sale and the resulting 800 Pounds were presented to Anne.

The next day, workmen came to take the bed away. They delivered it to an empty field several miles away and hence out of Stratford's view, and then, following William Shakespeare's express orders, the loyal lawyer touched a torch to the rushes piled on all sides, and the bed went up in flames. They watched it burn with a golden glow that subsided into russet coals.

Note: double quotation marks denote lines taken from Shakespeare. Single marks have been used for dialogue. Poetry by the author has no quotation marks.

A Manual of Arms

I

En Parade

We once were rough and tumble lads.
Who tarnished all at home,
But now we march to victory,
With Maréchal Vendôme.

By the King's hand, at Our Chateau of Versailles.
The sixth of February, in the year of Our Lord, 1706.

The soldiers arrayed for inspection today in the Place d'Armes were lucky. Both Suns shined upon them. The clouds enshrouding France of late have parted, thus might Apollo's rays mingle with Our own. The duc de

Vendôme, fresh from his Italian victories, would show off his troops, or at least the cream thereof. We made them wait a bit, for should not the monarch meet his army's expectations of glory? Tailors, valets and *perruquières* fussed forever in the line of duty, yet one must not let one's army wilt. At length We came out upon the balcony, saluted a welcome to the accompaniment of soldiers' cheers, and then, seeing Our steed brought up below, descended. We waved aside the waiting lackeys and their gilded stool, certain that the troops should see their King mount unattended. Our heralds blew the fanfare, and We rode out to greet the maréchal of the moment.

Vendôme is a man of straightforward albeit often boorish aspect. Would that Monsieur, Our royal brother, might at times exhibit some of the same raw gusto. Unfortunately, both men share a propensity for the secret sin. Vendôme at least is not the painted, fattened fop that Monsieur has become. Nonetheless, la Maintenon, in her enthusiasm to make Our court more moral, would have Us banish the duke for his reported sodomitic liaisons. We keep reminding her that winning battles may have a value at least equal to that of reforming sinners.

On seeing our approach, Vendôme descended from his carriage—it is said that he hates to ride a horse. How strange for a general, but given his proclivities, perhaps his nether regions are sometimes too tender. He came forward to greet Us with a deep bow, whereupon We also dismounted out of the usual consideration for courtesy, so that We might stroll with him to the viewing stand. A few pleasantries, and afterward he raised a scarf and let it fall. A charming signal. First must the twelve men of the duke's special guard bring forth the Austrian standards captured at—oh, some God-forsaken Italian place—and drop them at Our feet. Then, once We had trod upon them and returned to the stand, would one of the many bands strike up a march.

Well-ordered troops of grenadiers and soldiers of the line, dragoons and hussars, voltiguers and chasseurs paraded by, all turning their heads and raising swords or lances in salute to Our person. It was a shining, ever-shifting sea of blue, white and gold which stirred up such a rising cloud of dust as to hide the far stables. Last came the artillery. Two dozen polished brass cannon—twelve-pounders—rumbled with their caissons, thundering behind the horse teams. Now must the dust engulf us all.

Yet there was a constant breeze—thus does Mars always seem to smile on Vendôme—so that the cloud had cleared in time for Us to walk down the line of troops.

One does this with great gravity, looking into the men's eyes, smiling rarely and checking all. The wise monarch finds but one mistake, therein seeming vigilant. To discover more might be construed as impolite. We swatted at some dust on one man's lapels, and thus served up royal duty. There was, alas, probably more dust upon Our own person.

The final tiresome moment of this ordeal militaire would have Us witness soldiers at their drill. We returned with Vendôme to the viewing stand. He inclined his head and another band played a slow march, whereupon the twelve men of his personal guard sauntered to the fore.

<u>Attention</u>! They stood in perfect line, and one could see that Vendôme's vanity had tricked them up with new yellow facings for the blue coats, a trifle more gold braid than We would think seemly, and from their black tricornes, three tall white plumes spread so as to resemble Our Fleur de Lys.

<u>Present Arms</u>! The twelve raised their muskets in perfect unison, and one might perceive that Monsieur le duc's personal guard had, as is to be expected, elegantly filled their new uniforms. All were tall—at least six feet—with shapely legs and good strong arms. Though We would wish them to have had the large, well-twirled mustaches which give many of Our other soldiers so fine and fearsome an aspect.

<u>Fix Bayonet</u>! Now did the twelve swirl their muskets with one hand in a great arc so that at last the butts were planted by their heels, while the other hands, lightning fast, reached down to take up the shining blade and affix it to the barrel. This marvel of a swish and click reminded Us of the automatons that delight Our palace rooms.

Then came the final flurry of commands—"Prime, Load, Present, Aim, Fire!"—alas, We cannot remember all of the manual of arms. But the result was a clock-work machine made of men, who nonetheless smiled with enjoyment, eyes twinkling with pride and love for their commander. As a wondrous finale, Vendôme reached into his waistcoat and withdrew a handsome watch.

"A trifling gift for you sire, so that you might time the following."

The duke set the works in motion and placed the gilded bauble in Our hands. Then he nodded to his sergeant, who proceeded to a rapid screaming of the commands. Thus in uncanny unison would the twelve picked men fire three volleys in the space of one minute! We hoped for once that English or Austrian spies might be in attendance, thus to strike fear into their monarchs' hearts with news of Vendôme's readiness.

The duke dismissed his troops, and We strode with him back to Our chateau for a collation and a conference regarding his next posting to Flanders. France is lucky indeed to have such men. We think Madame de Maintenon must be left to stew a while longer in her moral soup..

II
En Marche

We are the twelve of Vendôme's guard,
Both <u>arrière</u> and <u>avant</u>,
Who stride beside his campaign coach,
And serve his every want.

——————

They call him Jolicœur, and it's the right name for him. For though his features are dark, he marches with a happy heart. The man ahead is known as Beausoleil, and that's a fitting name too because of the blond hair and bright smile that make him seem so sunny and chipper. Striding behind is Bonhomme, and he's a good man to have at your back. You can always trust him.

No soldier goes by his real name these days, preferring to be known by a nom de guerre. In fact, at morning muster when the sergeant calls out "Jean-Paul," Jolicœur sometimes has to stop and think just who that is.

He's happy to be on the road again, even if it is only for a two-day march west to the Duke's chateau. Most of the soldiers of Vendôme's army will be twiddling their thumbs at bleak barracks in Versailles or hot bivouacs on the champ de Mars in Paris. Jolicœur would rather have the sun on his back and the wind in his face. He also likes the sound of the mounted band that leads the little procession, though he hates dodging the droppings left by the horses of the cavalry troop which rides next in line. It might be worse though. He could be marching through the cloud of dust at the rear, behind all of those wagons that carry the duke's servants, his kitchen and tents, and the big rumbling one loaded with the booty so recently "appropriated" from Italy.

"No, thank you," thinks Jolicœur, having a care for the new plumes on his hat while shifting his pike across to the other shoulder, "I'll take my place here, striding beside his campaign coach."

And what a coach! Not spiffed up with gold garlands and painted panels like the duke's town coach. Well, it wouldn't do for a maréchal's carriage to present a shining invitation for the enemy's artillery. No sir, this one was downright dull on the outside: drab brown leather facings and black tack. But the inside was amazing. Silk cushions. Cunning little trays and tables, which fold out for food or drinks, or writing orders and accounts. There are also lots of hidden compartments for oh-so-many things, plus a trap door in the canopy so that the duke can stand on one of the benches, spread his maps out on the carriage top, and then scan the battlefield with his long brass telescope.

Jolicœur and all of the others of the duke's special guard know this because they are the only members of Vendôme's army who ever get to see the inside of the coach. This is the result of his penchant for "private inspections." Now, once more on the march, all twelve are wondering who will receive the first summons of the day.

Not long to wait. They hear the signal. It's the sound of a maréchal's baton rapping on the ceiling of the coach. Up on the driver's seat the coachman's helper puts his ear to a speaking tube, and swings around to call out, "Jolicœur," who turns with a wink, hands his pike off to Bonhomme, and then runs over to the door of the coach. He raps, hears "Enter," removes his tricorne (so that the damn plumes will not be crushed) and jumps through the door of the still moving coach, to sort of stand (head crouched to one side because of the low ceiling) in front of Louis-Joseph, duc de Vendôme and maréchal de France.

"Sit."

"Merci, My Lord."

"Undress."

"Mais oui, My Lord."

They all call him "My Lord" or "Your Highness." He insists on that.

Jolicœur removes his jacket, and folds it neatly to lie on the left of his bench. The duke sips chocolate from a porcelain cup. The guardsman undoes his jabot and starts on the many buttons of the waistcoat. The Duke sips more and looks on through half closed eyes. Jolicœur slips off his belt, and lifts the shirt up over his head. Only his britches and boots remain. He knows to wait now for the lord's command.

"Avant, I think."

"Oui, My Lord."

And Jolicœur, still sitting on the bench, spreads his legs wide so that his boots reach out to the far corners of the carriage floor, then springs up to grab the two straps that hang on either side just above the curtained windows. His body is stretched in an "X" now. A maréchal and a private regard each other in expectant silence.

The private sees a rather rumpled man perched on just the other side of fifty and just this side of paunchy. Vendôme takes a final sip and sets the cup aside. Cold blue eyes appraise from beneath the dark curls of a mountainous peruque. Dry lips smile thinly beneath a rather puggish nose. The burgundy velour coat is open to reveal a gold- embroidered waistcoat straining at buttons behind a deep blue sash that drips with jeweled military orders. Below, beige satin britches are stuffed into high black riding boots. This portrait of portly and rough aristocratic power is finished off by golden backlight streaming through the undraped oval rear window that perches above the Duke's wig like a hastily painted halo

The Maréchal sees that which pleases most, for the same golden light falls across the sturdy body of an active, youthful Gascon peasant just this side of twenty. Jolicœur's jet-black hair is shoulder length, but it's tied back with a ribbon in a proper military queue. It has a sheen that matches his polished black boots. Strong dark brows shade deep brown, sparkling eyes. High cheekbones frame an aquiline nose. Full lips are pursed in anticipation. In fact, the peasant has the more aristocratic face. And the body, "Oh what a landscape," thinks the duke, "and what a fine field for action!" Long, well-rounded arms reach out from wide shoulders, and the torso descends in a sinuous "V." Oh, such a perfect sight.

He sits up, smiles more broadly, and reaches forward toward Jolicœur's britches. Vendôme personally designed these uniforms. And his cleverest gambit was to have the tailors make the britches after an old, out-dated pattern, one that employed separate leggings with overlapping flaps both front and back so that just two buttons held all together. With the right hand he undoes a button over Jolicœur's right buttock. The left releases the button to the right of his groin. Then he peels the leggings down over the splayed boots, thereby revealing the private's privates, which lurk at the center of this most delectable "X."

Now the duke sits back again, relaxing into the swaying of a well-sprung coach. He always takes his time at first. Jolicœur knows this and equally enjoys the fact of searching eyes. He knows that the duke is watching his member sway from side to side below, and seeing his balls bounce along with the coach.

The cold blue eyes are warming now, raising to reconnoiter the battlefield, to seek out hills and valleys, and choose the method of attack, while shining Gascon eyes are waiting to see which of four leather cases will be taken out from below the Maréchal's seat. "Ah," thinks Jolicœur with some relief, "it's the green one." He knows that the others—red, blue, and black—hold equipment that makes more strenuous demands.

Vendôme sets the case on the bench to his left and opens it. Inside, nestling on a bed of green velour, are six instruments with elegant gold handles. He takes up the first pair. They are about two feet long—small riding crops tipped, of course, with short, supple leather straps.

"In classic fashion," says the Maréchal, "cavalry will lead off the attack." The private laughs to himself. He's been here before.

With a crop in each hand, the duke begins by trotting in along the arms, lightly stinging the shoulders, reining in at the valley of the clavicles, and then dividing his cavalry once again to canter over the smooth plains of Jolicœur's chest. He stings the nipples then rides down the left and right flanks, tapping ever faster and more sharply. The guardsman's breathing keeps apace, quick shallow breaths as the crops tap back and forth across the low foothills of his stomach. The duke taps lower, sidestepping the dark pubic forest that surrounds the ultimate goal.

Soon the crops gallop their way down the outer flanks of thighs as a diversion preparatory for the real charge, which is a mad, stinging rush up the tender inside of the legs. Jolicœur's chest is heaving now. His eyes shut tight, teeth clenched, waiting for the tabs to strike his balls. They do, and he gasps as the duke laughs, tapping the penis, watching intently as it begins to grow and stiffen.

"There's always a weakness at the postern gate. You must steel yourself, Jolicœur, for the future assault. But now it's time for the light infantry."

He sets aside the crops, to take up two other rods. They're tipped with feathers. And Jolicœur does have to steel himself. He can take the stinging crop or even the duke's whips, but the feathers drive him to distraction. He closes his eyes, knowing that Vendôme will start with the face. And he does, feathers stroking eyelids, gliding over cheek bones, then flitting down the sides of the neck. Already little beads of sweat are beginning to form on Jolicœur's brow.

As the feathers float over his Adam's apple, the private holds even harder to the leather straps, for he knows what will come next. They split and whirl across his chest, like little dervishes dancing on his tits, and then—oh, how he hates this—they dive into his armpits and flutter up and down his ribs. He wants to giggle now, but can't. The duke demands silence. The sweat is running down across his eyes, and OH GOD how he pulls upon the straps.

And Vendôme loves to watch those arms become long trembling ropes of steel; loves to see the sweat glaze Jolicœur's cheekbones, and then drip down along his chin and neck; loves those little gasps that he knows want so badly to be fevered, nervous laughter.

Now the feathers flit up and down across the stomach muscles, and the private's gasps become staccato heaves. He feels them flying over the smoothness of his groin and then around to tickle his pubic hair, diving lower to that damned inner skin of his thighs. Jolicœur freezes, holding his breath as the feathers rise to his balls. He can't help it. A huge gasp follows. He's stabbing at the air now as the feathers find their ultimate goal, sliding oh-so lightly out and back along his rigid organ and then—he's moaning, keening—as they dance endlessly around the flushed and silken tip.

The duke knows exactly when to stop. Jolicœur is left sagging, yet still trembling as he gasps for breath. His body shines with sweat.

"And now, arrière."

"Oui, My Lord."

He turns away, spreading his legs wide again, and grabs the straps. The duke takes another sip of chocolate. "This field may be even lovelier," he thinks as he sees the bunched muscles of a sweat-glazed back plunge down to perfect rounded cheeks.

"I shall now use the artillery."

"Oui, my Lord."

Jolicœur knows that this means the fifth tool, the little cat-of-nine-tails. It's a remarkable whip—God only knows what the strands are made of—which will sting like hell yet never leave a welt. He steels himself.

"Thwack," comes the first salvo, striking the tops of the deltoids.

"Rata-tat-tat," goes an endless barrage across his back.

"Thwap," and "thwap" again as flanking fire strikes his ribs and curls around to sting his chest. Jolicœur's body jerks each time. He's raised on his toes now. But silence is still the rule. There's much more to come. The Maréchal likes his battlefields to be rosy. The whip returns to the back, working its way down to those two lovely well-rounded cheeks. Thwack and thwap, over and over, and rich red beds of roses. The duke is pleased now. The field has been properly softened up.

"It is time, dear boy, for the engineers to mind their trade."

"Of course, Your Highness."

Jolicœur sags now, and his red ass arches back. The last tool will be tipped with an ivory egg.

"Our little battering ram," chuckles the duke.

Then the private feels it at the portal of his ass—cool and smooth and round—entering, spreading him, passing in to find that secret spot, moving forward and back, like the great breaths that enter and leave his lungs.

"Our advance guard," whispers the duke, as his finger enters to explore.

Soon Jolicœur feels prickling points, cool against his fevered back. They are the medals that decorate the Maréchal's sash. Then his voice becomes a hoarse whisper directly into Jolicœur's right ear, accompanied by pungent fumes of chocolate.

"And now we conquer all."

He feels the Maréchal enter him, thinks absurdly of how dogs grow to resemble their owners, and—though he has only felt but never seen the duke's organ—knows they share the same qualities: thick, grasping, pugnacious, and undeniable.

As the ramming builds, Vendôme holds tightly to the private's hips. Then his hands, wreathed by lace and the over-sized cuffs, rise up to tweak Jolicœur's tits. And at the last, one hand grabs the private's queue, holding on as with a horse's mane, while the other reaches around to stroke his organ. Imagine that, a duke seeking to give some pleasure in return! His hand slides along Jolicœur's penis, feeling its long slender flushed excitement. Does he realize that this one seems more graceful...perhaps even aristocratic?

No. Neither man can think of anything right now beyond...

And they both give a whoop of...

Well, anyway the coachmen hear it, and laugh and shake their heads. And the other guardsmen march on while raising their pikes in salute.

Jolicœur is dressing himself. The duke is wiping off his tools and replacing them in the green case. Then he reaches into a small leather bag and tosses a coin to the private, a gold ecu.

"Merci, my Lord."

"Send in Beausoleil," says Vendôme, as he places the green case back below his bench. Jolicœur smiles as he sees the duke take out the red case. Then he bows as best he can under the low ceiling, and jumps down from the coach. Bonhomme tosses him the pike, and Jolicœur is back on the march.

"He wants you now, Beausoleil."

The blond guard hands off his pike and rushes to the door. Jolicœur grins for he knows that the red case contains five graduated dildos. The last one is huge. Beausoleil will not be so chipper on the march this afternoon.

III
En Manœuvers

We do the manual of arms
With élan and panache,
And also demonstrate our charms,
Unbuck-e-ling our swash.

———

To begin with, the place was conceived as a love-nest. The Chateau d'Anet had been constructed over a century and a half before so that the lovely Diane de Poitiers could dally in the arms of King Henry IV. It was forty-five miles west of Paris, just far enough to evade the eyes and ears of a jealous and vengeful queen. No expense had been spared. Philbert de l'Orme served as the fanciful architect, and the great Benvenuto Cellini had provided decorative sculptures. His <u>Nymph of Fountainebleau</u> emulated Diane's sinuous form as it reclined in bas-relief over Anet's gate. The initials "H" and "D" were entwined all over the place.

Louis-Joseph, duc de Vendôme, who had inherited the estate some two decades past, would happily have changed the bas-relief to a sleeping satyr—or better a recumbent Hercules—but he had other, more expensive goals in mind in order to make his own love-nest of Anet. First, his architects had cut up many of Diane's great halls into suites of bedrooms for the many male guests that the duke desired to entertain. Second, the balustrade of the new staircase had its share of "L's" entwined to become "V's." And third, the great André le Nôtre had been hired to sweep away the old tight geometric gardens in favor of a more expansive plan. A Grand Canal allowed for punting or other aquatic pleasures, and even better, three long radiating allées had been cut through the forest which led to hidden gardens, suitable for secret trysts. Though here men did not have to hide from women, for the duke's establishment was mostly masculine. Still, those secluded forest bosquets offered delicious retreats for the acts of buggery that he so loved.

These many alterations had been expensive. Great estates ate money. Thank God for the Italian bullion. And now he must plan for a costly grande féte less than one week away and just a few days before his departure for Flanders. Ah, but this one might prove profitable if only the duke could find a way to win the wager. After all, the loss of a thousand Louis d'Or would be no trifle, but the possibility of winning two thousand —that would be a lovely triumph. And this was how the wager came about.

After visiting with the king at Versailles, Vendôme had paid a courtesy call on a dearer friend, the king's brother, at his chateau of Saint Cloud. There the duke found himself interrupting an argument between Monsieur and the marquis d'Effiat over which lord's "followers" had the most talent. Monsieur maintained that some of his young pages were good enough to have danced in the King's Ballet du Cour. D'Effiat sang the praises of his "Enfants" who might have starred at the Opera.

Then the wagering started. Vendôme could not resist. He was the one who raised the bidding to a thousand, and then sealed the bet by offering his own chateau as a stage for the contest. The theme of the performances, of course, must be one of male love.

But later that night, as he rode back to join his troops, the duke suddenly realized the one weak spot in the stratagem to which he had been led by his own greed. Where was Vendôme's talented corps of performers? His valets, cooks, and stable boys were good at their jobs, and most were handsome. That last, of course, had been one of the requirements. But performers? No, not at all. He had no private theatre at Anet, not even a house orchestra, as did so many others of his class. What to do? What to do?

Yet yesterday, while riding (among other things) to Anet in his carriage, the duke had found his answer. His private guard had very useful talents, if only he could train and rehearse them in time. Five days to win a wager. Hmmm.

Most of the duke's military escort had been billeted in the village. They would play no part in the festivities five days away, except possibly to guard the gates or ride sentry duty around the outer walls of the estate. But the twelve personal guards had been lodged upstairs, beneath the high-peaked eaves of Anet. Now, at their morning muster in the stable yard, Jolicœur and the others would hear their sergeant speak of a summons. One hour hence, they were to meet the duke in the guardroom of the chateau.

"Full dress uniforms, lads. All spit and polish."

The maréchal sat on a gilded arm chair. A pot of chocolate was steaming on a table to his left. Behind his right shoulder stood Alberoni, the fat, obsequious little Italian prelate who had become his majordomo. On the far side of the guardroom were lined up twelve clothes racks, each matched with a three-legged stool. When a tall case clock struck ten, they heard a drumbeat and the tramp of soldiers marching down the grand staircase and along the corridor.

"Open the doors, Alberoni. And close them after the guard have entered. Then go away and see to the arrival of my other guests. I shall ring this bell when I want them."

"But of course, Your Most Gracious and Sublime Highness," said a bowing Alberoni, who wished so badly that he could stay.

The twelve marched in behind the drummer boy and their sergeant, who called them to a halt, to right face, and then to attention, so that at the last each had stopped by one of the stools. Alberoni looked so sad and wistful as he closed the doors.

"Well, my fine Lads, we've been through much together," rumbled the Maréchal, as he stood to address his troops. "You have been brave and loyal, you have mastered the manual of arms to perfection, and you have pleased me in so many, many ways, not least in the wearing of these new uniforms.

"But now you must learn a new set of maneuvers. You are all going to be performers, my lads. Performers upon a stage."

They did not laugh, at least not audibly. But the Duke did. He couldn't help it. He roared with laughter. Then Beausoleil turned his head just a bit to wink at Jolicœur who tittered just a bit, and soon all twelve were laughing _with_ their Maréchal at his marvelous joke. Even the sergeant broke down and began to laugh.

"But its no joke," roared the duke, as he snapped his riding crop hard on the sergeant's thigh. The twelve snapped to a rigid attention, eyes firmly front, faces washed completely clean of mirth.

"In five days my gardens will be the scene of a trio of theatrical perfomances. One troop of dancers will be under the patronage of Monsieur, the king's brother. Another will sing under the auspices of the marquis d'Effiat. YOU will be my performers. And the patron of the best troop will win a wager that pays two thousand Louis d'Or. Win that wager for me and each of you shall have ten Louis. Lose it and you will march to Flanders behind the wagon train.

"Now, undress."

The twelve, still staring straight ahead, took off their coats and hung them on the racks. They sat as one, undid jabots, unbuttoned waistcoats, removed shirts, and hung them. Then unified automatons sat there waiting.

"Britches and boots too."

When they had finished, the duke called out "Attention!" and twelve well-formed naked men stood ramrod straight, bare feet planted on the cold marble floor. This was new. This was a mystery to them.

Now the Maréchal walked the line as though at an inspection, flicking his crop here and there on shivering thighs and stomachs. When the duke reached the end of the line, he turned and came back, tapping each man's organ in turn.

"We are going to learn a new manual of arms. But first a little demonstration."

He stood by his chair and rang the silver bell. Alberoni opened the doors, gawking from the corridor, and four of the duke's hunting hounds ran in.

"Come." They did.

"Sit." They did.

"Lie down." This too.

"Sit up." And that.

The duke crossed to his table to snatch four cuts of beef. He balanced one on each dog's nose, saying, "Hold," then sauntered slowly away, around the room, behind his twelve nude guards. The dogs may have twitched a bit, but they held. The Duke consulted the case clock and waited for a full two minutes to pass by.

"Take!" And the dogs flipped up their noses and thereby the meat, then caught it in the air. The duke, now standing by the doors, opened them, gave a whistle, and the chewing dogs raced out, nearly knocking over Alberoni in their haste. Vendôme laughed and slammed the doors in the prelate's face.

"That lads, is training. It is achieved by a combination of reward and punishment. Of pleasure and pain. Now I shall see to your training."

IV

La Victoire

Monsieur le duc takes care of us,
And we return the favor.
No other troops compare with us,
Whose lances never waver.

———————

Four days later, the birds of a feather had flocked together at the love nest named Anet. Monsieur Philippe de Bourbon, the king's brother, was as flushed and florid as an overfed rooster, while the marquis d'Effiat stood blanched and elegant like a high-strung egret. They sipped sunset champagnes on the garden terrace of the chateau. One mountainous wig of beribboned russet bobbed in consultation with another that was tightly curled of a silver gray, for the two men were utterly mystified. Just yesterday their separate wagon trains had arrived. Monsieur's procession had included his voluminous coach as well as six more carriages for the cast of twenty-four winsome gamins. To say nothing of three heavy drays loaded with scenery, costumes and workmen. D'Effiat's train had not been quite as large, for his "Enfants Précieux" numbered only eighteen.

Their respective troops had worked all day to set up the stages. Even here on the terrace one could hear the continuing racket of hammers and the yaps of workers' catcalls. Monsieur had been assigned the left allée, the marquis the right. Vendôme took the center one. And this was the mystery, for as far as they could observe while peering into the lengthening shadows, no preparations what-so-ever had been undertaken in that center avenue of trees. Monsieur kept sweeping the length of it with his little jeweled telescope. Nothing. What could their host be up to?

A third bird was hurrying back from the first allée. This was the chevalier de Lorraine, who served as Monsieur's majordomo—some said his procurer—but others called him the real master of Philippe's world. He was dressed with a more somber elegance in sleek black satin, even to the britches—a raven amidst the ruffled flock.

"Your stage is almost done, Philippe," said the chevalier, omitting both bow as well as obsequy, and thus confirming rumors of his upper hand. "Tomorrow morning we'll try to get our performers to practice with their hooves. I dread it, for they will carp and snap as is their constant want."

"Ah, but you will manage all," rejoined the rooster. "You always do."

"No help from you, Monsieur, yet I shall win your wager, as indeed I always have."

"Hooves?" said the egret, with an earnest twitch.

"A surprise, marquis, as all wagers should be," sniffed the raven, as he took away Monsieur's goblet and drained it.

"Oh look!" chirped the king's brother, as he peered through his telescope, "Vendôme is up to something."

Lorraine snatched the jeweled telescope. There was the Duke, in the shadows of the far end of the center allée, talking to several workmen. Two were digging a line of little holes. Another pair took up what looked like pots from a wheelbarrow and placed them in the holes.

"Is he planting a garden?" asked the rooster.

"No, silly fool, he's laying mortars for fireworks," sneered the raven. Then he watched the duke stride forward. "Why is he moving his fingers in that strange manner?" asked Lorraine of no one in particular, "Oh, I see, he's counting paces. How perplexing."

Halfway down the darkening tunnel of trees, when the duke had finished pacing, several footmen came out of the shadows with ladders. Others carried what looked like lanterns.

"What now?" mused the chevalier. "Ah yes, chandeliers and foot lights. Next, I assure you, we will see his stage."

But they saw nothing more. The workmen packed up their tools and trudged back to the stables. Vendôme resumed his forward stride to be met by a boatman who ferried him across the Grand Canal, whereupon, straight as an arrow, he made for his guests on the terrace. Here was the fourth bird—a rumpled, self-satisfied owl.

"Waiting till the last minute, are we, Vendôme?"

"Oh, all will be ready in time, Monsieur."

"But what of your stage, Louis-Joseph?" said Effiat.

"I shall leave that to le Nôtre and Mother Nature."

"I hope you don't live to regret it," murmured the chevalier, "for Monsieur has enlisted the talents of the great Torrelli to create his stage."

"And I have rented one entire from the Comédie Italienne," sniffed the marquis.

"Why gentlemen," crowed the owl, "I thought our goal was that of art without artifice. Come, come, my friends. I have a light super set up for us in the grand salon. Tomorrow is another day."

Tomorrow bloomed at Anet and found the two troops hard at work in secret behind the closed curtains of cardboard prosceniums. The marquis's string quartet played old opera songs by Jean-Baptiste Lully, and sometimes a human note or two would warble through. And from the other side came strange clumping sounds to the accompaniment of a grander orchestra playing new music by François Couperin. But little had happened in the center allée. The chevalier knew this because he had hidden several spies along its length.

"Nothing, Chevalier," said one of them, shortly after noon, "except to string wicks from the mortar pots and set up some rocket racks behind them."

"No, Chevalier," said another in the late afternoon, "Just some footmen placing the same three chairs as at the other two stages. They made jokes about the big chair being for Monsieur's derrière."

The raven cursed, for he hated surprises. Winning was always the product of careful cheating. What good would it do to sabotage fireworks or overstuffed chairs?

Sunset came, and all repaired to the chateau for the evening's banquet. The final bird, a little red would-be-cardinal, lurked behind. "Ah, Alberoni," said the raven, "we must talk."

The banquet was a huge success. Monsieur found the groaning board grand enough for gorging, and the marquis discovered delicacies delightful enough for his refined tastes. The Duke was pleased to see Monsieur's pages and d'Effiat's Enfants drink far too much in light of their ensuing performances.

"But Louis-Joseph, where are your performers?" asked the rooster with a burp.

"Shy," replied the owl, "being new at all of this."

And indeed, in a secluded gamekeeper's cottage at the far end of the forest, the twelve and their sergeant had spent these two days in endless practicing, except for those moments when a little wagon from the chateau kitchen rolled up, laden with good food and wine.

The chevalier now took his place at Monsieur's side, and whispered, "Not to worry, Philippe. A little bird has told me that our host will use common soldiers from his own army. Imagine, raw peasant performers! While we employ pages garnered from the very best of families." The raven smiled. "And in the end, blood will always win out."

"But what will they perform?"

"Alas, Monsieur, my confidant could not tell me that. Bawdy barracks ballads, I surmise. What else could such creatures know?"

The duke rapped his goblet with a knife. "Gentlemen, the sun has set. It is time for the revels to begin. To your places all."

As host Vendôme was delighted to go last in the order of performance. D'Effiat would lead. A carriage took the three to the southernmost allée, where gilded chairs awaited them. Precedence decided all. Monsieur as a prince of the blood sat center in the widest and certainly strongest chair, one that might have seemed a sofa. Duke and Marquis sat left and right. They, not counting a few serving men (who after all really did not count) were to be the only audience.

Servants rushed to touch their tapers to the footlights. A pretty little proscenium glowed with cascades of pink cupids, flitting at the top to hold a banner, which once said "Les Comédiens du Roi," but had been hastily repainted to read "Chansons d'Amour." The curtain represented a Zeus who was too rather feverish in his fondling of Ganymede.

The marquis rose and crossed to stand in front of his little stage.

"There you have it, gentlemen," said the egret, pointing above with a nervous hiccup. "We have (hic) adapted our great Lully's songs to themes of male love through (hic) history. May I pre(hic)sent 'Les Enfants d'Amour'."

Six hands clapped as the curtain rose to reveal a real Zeus and Ganymede in front of a cardboard forest. One must understand that the "Enfants" were not children, but young Parisian gallants who fluttered in the marquis's circle.

This Zeus warbled a Lully lullaby with new lyrics involving such as "rosy cheeks and love's fond tweeks." The singing, alas, matched the rhymes. Monsieur clapped politely but loved seeing the real cheeks more than hearing the sung ones.

And thus it went. Twelve songs, twelve pairs of historic lovers, and two dozen skimpy chitons that luckily slipped now and then to reveal winsome chests or rosy cheeks. Pretty, but hardly Priapic. The raven smiled as he weakly applauded. The duke nodded off. The marquis saw only his dear boys and beamed with pleasure.

The duke and his guests moved onward to the next display.

The great Giacomo Torrelli had done the rooster proud, especially when one realized that only one week's notice had been given. The old designer had dusted off some pieces from the cellars of the *Salle de Spectacles* and had them quickly touched up for the new theme. Overhead, two satyrs—rampant, of course—held aloft Monsieur's convoluted coat of arms. On either side a huge Hercules held up his side of the proscenium and his nether region displayed a Herculean fig leaf. There was no curtain now and no side scenery, only a grand, semi-ruined Greek temple at the rear.

Monsieur trundled to the fore, and burped.

"You must excuse me, gentlemen. Perhaps I enjoyed our host's table too much. Ah, well. First I must thank monsieur Torrelli and our young composer, Couperin, for working in such fevered haste on our behalf."

He burped again while six hands clapped with feigned politesse. "Tonight my lovely pages will present a ballet entitled, 'The Battle of the Lapiths and the Centaurs,'"

Then he bowed and burped his way back to his seat.

Flutes played a dainty shepherd's tune. A dainty Lapith "girl" entered, plucking dainty flowers at the footlights and placing them in a dainty ribboned basket. Then drums boomed and thunder sheets rumbled along with the clump of hooves on planks as twelve Centaurs galloped to the stage. Would that their torsos had been as burly as their wood and canvas hindquarters. Would that their real legs had been strong enough to move the levers attached to the paper maché rear ones. Alas, these horsy rumps were dragged about the stage much like ladies' trains are kicked and swished about the dance floor. The ensuing maiden's rape was, well, to be kind, ungainly. Deep bleats of horns and low weeping strings provided additional drama as the centaurs struggled to bear off the maiden as well as their horsy butts.

New strains of flutes warbled bucolically with violins. Twelve handsome Lapith youths danced forward from the columns of the temple. They leaped about in short tunics, and thereby revealed a bottom or two, until their pastoral joy was banished by the discovery of the basket of flowers abandoned at the footlights. "Oh horror!" screamed the music. "Oh ghastly deed," said the dancers' gestures. And then was heard the piteous far off wail of the maiden. Leaping Lapiths charged off stage.

There was applause of sorts.

The rooster was beside himself—if that be possible—with joy. The egret sat erect with jealous interest, the raven smiled serenely, and the owl happily snored.

Now hunting horns blared forth. The centaurs galloped on with their purloined maiden. Aha! More instruments joined the fray, and vengeful Lapiths leaped in from the wings. Limbs, both real and maché leaped and kicked and ripped and cracked. One horse butt, no, two were thus immobilized. But best of all some tunics were ripped away. The maiden was saved, and one randy page seemed to be humping a horse as the curtain fell.

"A triumph, Monsieur," cooed the egret, "surely you will win."

"My thanks to the chevalier," crowed the rooster, "for once again you have done me proud."

"Evermore," quoth the raven, "at your service."

"Ah, but wait, my friends," chortled the owl, "for I believe that we must see one other perfomance."

———

And now the guests are seated in the center allée, seeing only a forlorn row of footlights and five flickering chandeliers that hang from the over-arching trees. They are no longer quite alone, for behind, scattered among the trees, are members of the first two companies. Quite a crowd, in fact. Even further back, Alberoni watches, having appropriated his master's long telescope. Ahead, the dark tunnel of trees stretches into black infinity.

The duke simply stands, holds his scarf high, and drops it.

They hear the distant sound of two snare drums beating out a lonely tattoo. Then a trio of figures materializes out of the far shadows. It is the sergeant, tightly flanked by two drummer boys. They are in full dress uniforms, marching straight ahead. They stop just behind the footlights. Then the sergeant barks out a command and the two boys march smartly left and right to the sides. The guests of honor can now see from the receding perspective of white plumes that twelve more men stand directly behind the sergeant. He barks out another set of commands, and now the guests gasp, for the twelve men march, splitting left and right to form a line across the footlights. They wear their boots, their tricornes with the plumes—and nothing else.

The sergeant says, "At ease," and the twelve stand with legs slightly apart and hands behind their backs.

And even Monsieur must admit that all twelve are so much more robust and handsome than any of his pages. D'Effiat is salivating at the sight. Lorraine simply narrows his eyes. A distant Alberoni has to wipe fog off of his telescope lens. The wayside members of the other casts applaud.

The duke simply says, "Sergeant, you may begin."

"Attention." And the men stand straight and tall.

"Present Arms." The drums begin a slow roll, and twelve penises rise erect in unison.

All are now applauding, except for the raven.

"Gentlemen," says the duke, "would you care to inspect the troops? Monsieur, you must lead."

The rooster levers himself up, betraying greater strength than usual, and waddles with Vendôme around the footlights to the right end of the line. The egret follows, and a far off Alberoni drops the telescope to wander forward in a helpless trance.

Monsieur looks the first man up and down. It's Beausoleil.

"Why what am I to do?" asks the king's brother.

"Inspect, surely." Says the duke.

"But?"

The duke takes the rooster's pudgy hand and guides it to Beausoleil's balls.

"Oh dear, how wonderful," sighs Monsieur, as he hefts.

Jolicœur is next in line, and the rooster is not now so reticent. He reaches out to feel the shaft, and shudders with joy. D'Effiat now holds Beausoleil. Lorraine remains back in his chair, stewing.

Just then the duke catches a glimpse of a red cassock forcing its way forward through the crowd behind the chairs.

"Why Alberoni, what are you doing here?"

The wide-eyed prelate stops in his tracks.

"Go back to the chapel and pray, dear boy."

Alberoni, face as flushed as his cassock, turns to leave. The duke smiles to himself. Bonhomme is next in line. And so it goes. Eventually, one might even say reluctantly, the guests of honor return to their seats. The sergeant calls "At ease," and penises begin to droop.

"And now messieurs," says a beaming maréchal, "the final maneuvers of our Manual of Arms. Sergeant, if you please."

"Attention." The men stand to.

"Present arms." The drums begin a roll as before, and twelve penises rise erect in unison again. But this time the drums beat to a different tempo, a wilder one of ever increasing speed. Behind, the sky rockets begin to soar.

"Load." Left hands begin to stroke.

"Ready." The men stiffen, and close their eyes.

"Aim." They throw their hips forward, and slightly tremble to the faster beat.

"And Fire!" And they do! Twelve men ejaculate in unison, sending white loops of "ammunition" in trajectories that arc forward over the footlights. Behind the mortar bombs explode high above.

By now all of the pages and enfants have crowded behind the three chairs and are applauding, whistling, catcalling wildly. The rooster and the egret are standing too, both cheering, both aware of a certain moisture seeping through their britches. They each hand a bag of one thousand *Louis d'Or* to the duke. He takes them with a grateful bow and nods to the sergeant.

"Salute." The twelve salute. More wild applause.

"To the center, march!" They march to the center and then away in single file. The sergeant and his drummer boys follow to disappear into the distant darkness.

Of course the party went on through the night, and all the halls and courts and bosquets of Anet were scenes of wild debauch. But the twelve did not attend. The duke felt that he had shared them quite enough thank you. The next morning all of the guests packed up their stages and nursed hangovers in too-swaying carriages on their way to Paris.

The day after that, the maréchal and his minions departed for Flanders. And once again, Jolicœur received the first "inspection."

Rope

Above all else in the wide world, Shandy Weaver loved rope. He cheered with joy, hugging the foremast shrouds of <u>The Rights of Man</u> as she sailed into Portsmouth Roads. His bare feet snuggled the blocks, the skin of his chest pressed into the web of the ratlines, and his arms entwined themselves in the stays like the tendrils of a voracious vine.

"Ah Billy, climb up and see the sights!" shouted Shandy to the blond sailor who lounged at the rail below. And Billy—oh the handsome sailor Billy—gave a whoop, and swung up behind his mate, feet snuggling the same blocks, arms entwined with his on the same stays, bare chest fair nuzzling Shandy's shoulder blades, and his face cheek by jowl, grinning in wonder, as the wind strove to weave their brown and blond hair together.

Thus Shandy's heaven—the salt breeze whipping by, hard rope straining in front, handsome Billy pressing behind, and fair Portsmouth off the starboard bow.

"Ah now Billy, it's a great city you'll soon be seein', an' I'll be the one to show it to ye. Every church spire and tavern of it. But best of all, I'll take ye to see the longest room in the world. The Rope-walk, laddie. A wonder 'tis. Nothin' like it anywhere."

Shandy's reverie was cut short by the first mate's call of "Hands to braces." He and Billy heaved away on foremast sheets to back the main, and after hearing "Anchor aweigh," they scurried aloft, happy monkeys swinging out on yardarms to furl the great sails. That done, they raced below to their hammocks on the lower deck, queuing up their hair, and ducking into their sea chests for the black, wide-brimmed hats and blue tops that Captain Graveling insisted upon for those who would man his gig.

Billy, though new to the sailor's life, had been appointed as one of these special rowers from the first moment that he stepped on board The Rights of Man. The captain loved Billy, not the way that Shandy did in his secret heart, but in the way that all shipmates love their handsome sailors. Who could not be fond of a man so fair and strong and—well—as down right good hearted as Billy Budd?

The two raced up to the ship's waist with their four other rowing mates, then all leaped to scale the gunwales and drop smartly into the gig. "Oars up!" The captain descended to sit in the stern with his first officer, who manned the tiller and gave the order: "Oars out, and pull away." And then they were off, plowing through the bright blue foaming waves to Portsmouth.

"Ye'll want to be the one who takes our business to the Rope-walk, now won't ye, Shandy?" said the captain as they docked, and Shandy nodded. He was handed a list of cordages. "And who goes with ye?"

"I'll go, Sir" piped Billy, "for I hear 'tis the biggest room in the whole world, and I would na' miss it."

"Aye," said the first officer, with a knowing wink, "and Shandy's just the one to show it to ye."

In any other port, an ordinary merchant captain like Graveling would have had to buy his cordage from a common chandler, but the captain knew that Shandy had a special friend who would let him purchase navy stores directly from the Rope-walk. And that was a better bargain any day.

———

One must stop here to consider that Shandy wore more than the captain's blue shirt and black hat, as well as those baggy muslin pants that all other sailors donned. Shandy's love of rope, and all the lore of rope, had bid him to create a special garment. It was a sort of cat's cradle of white cotton twine, which wound around his torso and over his shoulders in a webbed masterpiece displaying every knot known to man. And then, unseen by any of his shipmates, the web descended even lower, strapping over his groin and snaking down between his buttocks to encase his privates in a tight cotton cage that, to Shandy, felt oh-so-good.

He had started making another of his rope shirts, one that he hoped someday to give to Billy. Shandy had already tendered him the handsomest of rope belts.

The two strode proudly through the streets of Portsmouth. Many a publican offered greetings as they passed, and many a doxie hailed to them from the gates of alleys. But they would have none of that. The Rope-walk called.

Shandy presented his compliments to one of the smartly garbed marines that guarded the gates of Portsmouth Yards.

"They look like lobsters," said Billy with a too-loud laugh, which Shandy shushed as they cleared the gates.

"There Billy, look'ee there!" said Shandy, pointing at a three-story brick building. "The King of France has a great mirrored hall that is but a hundred and fifty feet long. But we English have this place—near ten times as big. The longest room in the world m'lad."

Billy stared and swore he could not see the end of it. Shandy marched him right up to the door, saying, "How d'ye do," to another marine, who answered "Why Shandy, old sod." Billy gulped at the realization of his shipmate's obvious importance.

"Those be the warehouses," said Shandy, pointing off to the left, "stuffed full of jute from India and hemp from the East Indies and everywhere else in the great world. Ah, that be the makings of strong ropes, Billy, the kind that stretch and strain and bind us to the wind"

Then they stepped through huge doors into the longest room in the world. And Billy thought his eyes might burst. His nose too, from the dry, musty aroma of hemp, and the stinging smell of hot tar. The place was forty feet wide, thirty high, and four hundred yards long. Great wooden trusses soared above. Golden dust filled the air and slanting rays of sun sliced through it from high windows, like an endless row of sharp, glowing sword blades stacked all the way to eternity.

Billy started forward, but Shandy took hold of his companion's broad shoulders to turn him to the left, then pointed out past his cheek toward doors that led to a sun-lit court.

"There be the hackling yard, Billy, where all those bales of hemp is combed, so to speak, pulled over sharp iron spikes, like shark's teeth mounted on boards. That way the fibers be strung out to make a yarn."

Now they turned back to see a row of six wooden wheels, graduated in size from no larger than the spinning wheel that Billy remembered from his mum's cottage, all the way up to bigger than the most giant of wagon wheels.

"And here's where it be spun, Billy," said Shandy, pushing his friend over to the smallest wheel.

"By my stars, 'tis Shandy," said a much older man who seemed to have a huge skein of fur wrapped around his waist.

"'Tis, Thomas, 'tis, and this be Billy, one of me mates, come to see the Rope-walk, and how the ropes is made."

"Well, Billy, me buck, stand back and watch."

One end of the long roll of hemp that was wrapped round Tom's back had a little loop tied in it, which he attached to one of three hooks mounted over the wheel. Then he stepped backward for about twenty feet, playing out a line of hemp and said "On you go, Johnny." Now a boy standing at the wheel pulled upon a crank and the wheel revolved, driving a leather belt, which made the hooks begin to turn. "Even strokes, Johnny, even," called Tom. As the loose line of hemp twisted and tightened, he walked backwards, playing out more and more fiber, until, some twenty minutes later, he held the end of a hundred feet of a twisted cord no wider than a child's little finger.

"That, Billy, is but one yarn," said Tom with a bow. "Three yarns can be twisted into a strand, three strands into a hawser, and tree hawsers to a cable. But it all starts here with me and Johnny."

Billy nodded with open-mouthed wonder. Shandy led him to the other ever-bigger wheels, where indeed yarns were woven across greater and greater lengths to form strands and hawsers and cables. "Look at the brawny strength it takes to make the sinews of a ship, for that is what ropes be, Billy-boy. The masts is bones, the sails be muscle, but it's the sinews that make all work. An' you and me be good sailors due to our own sinews.

"Our mate Red Whiskers thinks he's strong for all the meat he carries. Butchers raised him, don't ya know, Billy? But two weeks ago, when he dared to be impertinent with ye—an' you decked him with a mighty blow—now where did all those blown up muscles get him? It was yer sinews, mate, that unleashed the power o' yer arm, which be round enough with muscle, yet not the bloated beef o' Red Whiskers."

"Oh, tha's all f-f-forgotten," answered Billy with the little stammer that always beset him in moments of emotion. "Now Red and me be b-b-best o' friends."

"Oh now he loves ye, mate. We all do. Aye, an' that's as it should be. Still it's sinews saved you. Look at me own arm, Billy. This bicep be long and stringy, but it's as hard as rope."

And it was true, for Shandy, at the age of thirty-two, had honed his body like the tautest rigging of a man o' war—not an ounce of fat; neck and thighs corded like hawsers; torso wound up to a tight cable; even toes and fingers woven like strands. And covering these sinews was a sun-tanned skin as hard and strong as the tarred stays of the shrouds. Oh. thought Shandy, it looked so good when seen through the cage of his rope shirt as to be a work o' sinuous art.

"Ah, but Billy be the real work o' art," mused the lean man, looking at his friend striding ahead, running a hand along a newly stretched cable. Billy were a man o' peace, and of a piece to delight the eyes of all the old Greek gods. A fine and rakish sloop he were. Backbone as straight as any mast. Muscles firm like tightly filled sails. Sinews taut and true. And skin—ah the fine glowing luster of a healthy twenty years.

Oh how good a rope shirt would look on *him*, and how grand it would be to see his privates straining in a rope cage. Shandy shook his head in wonder at the thought and then remembered their business here at the Rope-walk.

"Now, Billy, ye'll meet the master of all this," said the mentor to his awed mate, as they ascended wooden steps to a high bridge that overlooked the far end of the world's longest room.

Gentleman Jack Straw stood bestride the bridge like Zeus on Mount Olympus. He towered over the two—a decade older than Shandy, a full head taller, and that head shaved and shining in the center of a sword blade of light. Coal-dark eyes glowed within the shadow of his face.

"Well Shandy, come to call for cordage once again?" said a voice as strong and dark and lightning sharp as a storm at sea.

"Aye, Jack, and this be my mate Billy."

"Come to see the Rope-walk, Billy? said Jack Straw with a searching look that Billy thought might burn into his soul. "And what have you learned?"

"Th-that r-rope be the sinews of a sh-ship, an' it p-please you sir."

"Oh it does, Billy, it pleases me," said Jack Straw with a dark wink to Shandy, "Now, Billy Boy, why don't you take yourself across the bridge to that far room? There's samples there of all the 'sinews' that we make."

"Aye, sir," said Billy, sidling gingerly around Jack Straw, and then sighing with relief as he near ran to the sample room.

"Is this a treat you've brought for me, Shandy?" Winked Jack, "For I should like to initiate him into the mysteries of rope."

"Ah no, Jack, not yet. But give me a voyage to tie a few knots with the lad, an' then we'll let him join the order."

"Good, Shandy. Do that, and then it might be that I'll just sit back and watch, to see how much you've learned."

They both smiled at the prospect.

"I suppose you'll be wanting to tie a few on tonight, Shandy?" Shandy nodded. "It must be so," continued Jack, "for tomorrow I've an admiral in tow. We'd best be rid of your handsome mate."

"Leave that to me Jack," said Shandy, as he crossed the bridge and entered the sample room. Billy looked up at rows of rope and display boards full of knots.

"A wonder 'tis, Shandy!"

"Aye, lad, 'tis indeed," said Shandy, "but now you must leave us, for I've bargaining to do with Gentleman Jack."

"Ah. I'll just wait then out there in the yard."

"No Billy, for he and me will raise a few, and spend near half the night in haggling. Ye'll have to leave."

A shadow crossed Billy's face.

"Now not to worry, mate, Just take yerself out to the gate where we came in, and then turn left on Shipping Lane an' find an ale house called *The Happy Anchorage*. Red Whiskers and all yer friends'll be there. An' then tomorrow night I'll show you all the town. I promise ye."

"But..."

"No buts. Be off with ye."

And Billy—handsome Billy—stepped down and out and across the yard and through the gate into fair Portsmouth. Jack and Shandy watched him from the bridge, winked and licked their chops, and turned in the opposite direction when they exited the gates.

Jack Straw lived alone in an old warehouse at the sea end of Shipping Lane. It was mounted on pilings, and its bolted door was approached via a narrow wooden walkway that creaked like the gangway of a ship. He made his rooms in the old offices on the first floor, but entertained a select group of friends in the high vast space above. Now a blindfolded Shandy preceded Jack up groaning stairs that led to the loft. They creaked for a good reason, just like the gangway did. Jack didn't like to receive surprises, though he enjoyed giving them. He guided Shandy to the center of the soaring room.

"You'll love this, Shandy. Made with you in mind, and now you'll be the very first to climb it. But first I think I should see your handiwork. I'll light some lamps while you reveal it."

While Jack lit two oil lamps Shandy took off his hat, and then the blue top, and his host gave an appreciative whistle. "That's well indeed, Shandy," said Jack as he came closer to finger the knots of Shandy's rope shirt. "But I would see what gives it such a mighty stretch." Then Jack lowered Shandy's muslin pants. "Oh ho, my friend, your cock strains so at its pretty cage." He reached behind to pull sharply up upon the twine that cleaved the cheeks, and Shandy sighed and raised up on his toes. "Oh, the poor caged cock. It's so excited Shandy. Ah, but wait till you see what awaits you. Then your well tied cage might burst."

That was when Jack Straw removed the blindfold.

Shandy let his eyes adjust as he scanned the familiar high brick walls, the tall shuttered windows, and the rails of belaying pins holding every kind of rope that had ever been made. He knew from past visits that other lines and pulleys descended from the rafters. Then Jack turned him to look at the opposite end of the room, and Shandy's caged cock leapt for joy.

Six sets of blocks were bolted to the wooden floor. Six pulleys led to other blocks from which shrouds stretched up to a point on the highest beam of the gabled roof, some sixty feet above. Tied across the six shrouds, every foot on up to the point, were the ratlines for climbing. But they did not end at the outer stays, extending instead to be gathered by other lines that pulled off to the sides of the room. These pulleys, plus the six below, had their own lines leading to a pin rail near by. Oh, the stretching that this could allow! It was a masterpiece of rope-work.

"Ah, Jack, ye've been a cunning spider."

"Indeed I have. Well, my fine fly...Climb aboard!"

With a whoop of joy, Shandy ran and leaped right up to the shrouds. Once again his bare feet nuzzled the topmost block of the outer stays, his chest rubbed into the grid of ratlines and his arms reached out above to grasp the edges of the wedge. He shook the whole grid of rope, humped the air through it, whooping as he swayed.

"Aye, now you've had your fun, my lithe fly. It's time to turn around and properly weave yourself in my web."

Shandy shifted his hands to a point high over his head, grabbed the ratline there, and swung his body around to face front. Then he pulled himself up and let his legs weave through the ratlines until his feet once again rested on the outer blocks. He repeated the process with his arms, threading them out and through the ropes so that he was truly woven, spread-eagled in Jack's wonderful web. Now Shandy's cock pressed so much upon the cotton cage as to be unbearable.

"Well wound, Shandy, but we shall, of course, weave more."

Then Jack Straw withdrew to a far corner and rolled forward his "working platform." A flight of steep wooden steps led to a six foot high perch, with a rail from which hung coils of various twines and rope.

"No sense climbing up those lines with you, Shandy, for soon you'll sweat buckets, and that would sully my apparel."

Indeed, Jack Straw would always retain his clothes during these sessions, the fine clothes of a gentleman: silken hose, velvet breeches, embroidered waistcoat, cravat, flared coat, everything except the powdered wig. There was also a gold ring piercing his right ear lobe. All in all, he was a dashing, if menacing, man. No one would ever dream of challenging him to a duel. Now he ascended his platform, and face to face, his eyes burned Shandy's smile away.

"We shall begin with your hair." Jack loosened the queue and took up shanks of the shoulder length hair, twisted, and tied them off to stays and ratlines. When he had finished, Shandy's head was immobilized by a halo of radiating tonsorial spikes.

"And now, my friend, the fingers." He snared each finger in a tight loop of twine, then tied them out, spread like the spikes of Shandy's hair.

"Toes too, don't you think?" And Shandy, whose head most certainly could not turn down, only felt the twine ensnare his toes.

Now Jack bent back to take up a coil of white cotton rope. "Best Virginia Cotton, Shandy. You'll remember the feel of it, and it looks quite smart encasing well-tanned limbs like yours." When he was done, interlaced spirals bound Shandy's legs and arms to the web.

"You've seen to your torso, Shandy, but look below. Ah no, of course you can't. But you can feel what I see: a cock that wants so very badly to be free." He stroked the sore-strained cotton cage, and Shandy writhed (as much as he was able). Then he opened it, and Shandy gasped to feel his privates stab out into the air. Next, Jack did that which always near-crazed an immobilized Shandy. He just blew upon the cock. It was as though sea breezes celebrated freedom, like the rigid bowsprit of a ship plowing out across cool water. And every time Jack blew, Shandy almost exploded.

"Ah Shandy, surely you know that a good rope should be whipped."

Shandy knew this well, and he knew that Jack did not refer to a Cat o' Nine Tails, but to the well-wound cylinder of twine that kept the end of a rope from unraveling. Jack began by whipping Shandy's ball sack. Tight at the top, and tighter on down to press the two orbs so exposed at the furthest possible extension. Jack blew upon them, but Shandy just gasped, filling his lungs, which strained against the taut rope shirt.

Then Jack began whipping Shandy's cock, talking to it all the while. "Oh, my rigid friend. (twine starting to wrap at the base) Enjoyed your freedom did you? (winding further) Stabbing into the cool breezes? (further) Oh you are the cock of the walk, you are. (tighter) No...I have that wrong. (almost up to the tender lips of the glans) You're the cock of the Rope-walk!

And Shandy couldn't help it. He shot a broadside upon Jack Straw's cravat.

"Shandy, Shandy, Shandy! Shame upon you. Ruined my best jabot, you have. Well there's nothing to it but to change. I think I'll eat and drink a bit too, leaving you to consider the error of your ways."

Shandy considered for an hour or more—and the cock of the Rope-walk never subsided from his urgent stiffness.

———

Of course the steps groaned when Jack returned. So did Shandy, but with keen anticipation.

"Ah Shandy, I feel so refreshed, and so I'm sure do you." Then he looked down. "Oh yes, your cannon has been recharged." Jack began at his pin rail. "Rigging should be taut, my friend. It's too bad that our sessions must be so private, don't you think? I should like to have some musical accompaniment right now. But what? Ah yes, a string quartet!"

Jack laughed, but alas there was a limit to Shandy's sense of wit. The rope-master tugged the lines that led to the six lower pulleys. Shandy felt his hair near tear at its roots. His heels rose and his toes screamed. Then Jack heaved upon the two remaining lines, the ones that spread out to the sides, and Shandy knew for sure what it might mean to be "one with the rope." The most wonderful sensation of all: Shandy's sinews tested, stretched to the very limit.

"And now, my ensnared one, has come that delicious time when we play the great game, and thereby gauge how successful your studies have been."

Shandy enjoyed a secret smile of both pride and relief, for he had, in careful private, in the deepest bowels of his ship, done his homework well.

"I think we may forgo the blindfold, for you're present coiffure will not allow any lowering of the eyes." Now Jack reached into a box to choose a short length of rope. He raised the unwhipped end to first stroke it along Shandy's left cheek; the strings of his neck; the well his throat; then lower to grind the whipped end on his tit; and at the last to envelope the frayed end over the exposed head of his penis.

"That be Virginny cotton," said Shandy in triumph.

"And right you are, Shandy. But that was easy. Try this."

"It be stringier," said Shandy, by the cheek. "Rougher too," by the tit. "And hint o' sap," the glans, "I knows it...Philippine hemp!"

"Good lad. And now another."

"That be (cheek) sharper, a bit (tit) crumbly, and (penis)...ah, there be a dry crispiness. 'Tis Indian jute."

"Well done, my friend. One more."

Cheek and tit told him little, but the soft exposed skin of his glans noticed the sharp end of a bristle or two. "Ah Jack, this be Jamaican hemp."

"Oh Shandy, you have studied well, and done me proud."

"Aye Jack," said Shandy with a glow, "Tis the product of many hours in the blackness of the bilge runnin' samples over me 'Cock of the Rope-walk' as ye so kindly called it."

"Ah but now I must present you with a wondrous mystery." Unseen, Jack was donning leather gloves. "Some two decades past, the famous Captain Cook returned to Portsmouth with the leaves of a hemp-like plant that he had found growing on an Island called Tahiti. Not long ago, I discovered the forgotten little bale in our warehouse, and had Old Tom spin out a yarn or two. It failed one test for good rope, and now, just for you, I shall demonstrate why."

Jack held up a short length of rope before Shandy's eyes.

"It be beauteous golden, Jack."

"Aye, Shandy. It does make the very prettiest of ropes." He ever so lightly used it to stroke along the cheek.

"And soft, Jack, softer by far than the Virginy cotton.

"Aye, again." Now he jabbed it upon the left tit, and Shandy gasped in pain as a hundred needles thrust into his tit.

"There you see, Shandy, is our problem, and hence my leather gloves. The fibers are so very sharp. But now we have the final test."

"Oh please Jack, not that, please."

"Ah poor Shandy. Surely you realize that all testing must be complete and without bias. Here goes, my hapless sailor."

Oh, did Shandy scream, as a thousand sharp needles entered the tip of his penis. His sinews overcame the strong ropes, to set up among them those singing vibrations that a ship knows only from the greatest of storm winds. His wails echoed from the walls like the songs of banshees, and sparks of Saint Elmo's fire coursed through his veins.

"There is also the acid nature of the sap. Most uncomfortable, I am told. You would seem to agree Shandy."

"Oh Jack, 'tis burning my very soul!" he whispered.

"Mayhap your soul could stand a bit of burning." Jack bent down to better observe his handiwork. "Oh Shandy, you should see the Cock of the Rope-walk now. His rosebud glows bright red and flashes with a thousand little seeming rays of golden sun. I know just the thing. I'll cool him."

Then Jack puckered his lips and blew, and Shandy, rigid in every fiber of his being, eyes bulging, heart thumping, breath heaving, mouth open, screamed a scream the like of which Jack, in all of his experience, had never heard.

"Aye lad, enough's enough. I'll rescue you." Jack went below to find some candles, while Shandy writhed and whimpered in his cradle of rope.

"The cure, my friend, may be as bad as the cause," said Jack, upon his return. The he took up a candle and dripped its hot wax on Shandy's left tit.

Shandy gasped, waiting for it to cool, then he screamed out again, as Jack flicked away the wax, and a hundred burning needles left his flesh.

"Good, good. That worked well enough," said Jack, "Now comes the harder part." He dripped the wax from four candles into a little pewter cup, and when it was full...

"Gird your loins, Shandy, that is if they aren't girded enough already." Jack raised the little cup, plunged the tip of the penis in it, and Shandy fainted dead away.

When all had cooled, Jack peeled away the wax cap, and then restored his friend to consciousness through the gentle act of spreading fine oil on his cockhead. Then Jack did something that he had never done for any other member of his 'ropist' order. He kissed Shandy's cockhead, enveloped its lips with his, kissed upward to his groin, his belly, his nipples, and at the last, lingered at his lips, and with his tongue, raped Shandy's mouth. Shandy's second broadside would ruin Jack's velvet breeches.

The next night a somewhat shaky Shandy took the handsome sailor Billy to see the church spires and alehouses of Portsmouth—and good to his word, every one of them. And Billy thought it to be the grandest night he had ever known. The next day, *The Rights of Man* weighed her anchor to set sail for the East Indies. And Shandy worked in fevered secret to finish the rope shirt.

Not long after, as their hardy ship prepared to leave the channel narrows and broach the wide Atlantic Sea, did Shandy Weaver invite Billy Budd to come below and see a treasure. And Billy—ever eager and trusting Billy—followed his mate to a lamp-lit nest behind the great water casks in the depths of the bilge. Here Shandy had set out upon his one good blanket a little feast of cheese and grog, purchased at a steep price from the master of the galley.

"Tis a landlubbers picnic, an' just for ye and me," said Shandy.

"Tha' be right kind o' ye," said Billy.

Both men had long ago doffed their sailor's muslin shirts, but Shandy, of course, retained his knotted pride and joy, which now, in the flicker of the two oil lamps, glowed bright against his deep brown skin.

"What think ye, Billy, o' me rope-tied shirt?"

"Oh 'tis a handsome piece o' work, Shandy."

"An think ye mayhap you would enjoy wearin' such a garment."

"Oh, to be sure, Shandy. But I could never have the skill to make one half as fine as yours."

"True, lad, but ye don't have to, for I've made one for ye."

And now did Shandy produce the fruits of his twiney labor. He laid it down in Billy's lap.

"Oh Shandy. I know not what to say!"

"Say nuthin' lad. Just put it on."

Whereupon did Billy rise and try to wriggle into the cat's cradle of cotton rope, and at the last Shandy helped him by tucking here and there.

"But what be th-these th-things for, Shandy?" asked the wearer, as he puzzled over the strings behind and the knotted bag in front.

"Ah, that be what holds her tight," said the maker, as he lowered his muslin pants to demonstrate. Billy stared below. Quizzical was the look.

"Oh fret not Billy. Let me show ye." Whereupon did he lower Billy's pants, who stood quite rigid now, as Shandy reached through and behind and brought the strings forward with one hand, and looped them through the bottom of the bag. Then he took hold of Billy's privates. Billy froze into a statue, while Shandy stuffed, and tied, and oh-so-slowly rose, in love with his handiwork, eyes seeing the bulging bag, the classic groin, the sculpted midsection, the wide planes of the chest and round shoulders—all bound in lovely rope—that fine neck, the jutting chin, the trembling lips.

Shandy couldn't help it. He kissed Billy full upon the lovely mouth. And Billy, without thought, rammed his arm forward. His fist met Shandy's chin and threw him up to smash against a far water keg.

"Sail on the port bow!" came a distant foretopman's cry.

Billy tried to take the shirt off, but of course the knots had been well tied, so he ripped it away, shredding it with all the strength in his body. Then he grabbed up his pants, saw that Shandy was out cold, yet breathing still, and ran for the gangway to the upper decks.

"All hands to quarters. Ready to welcome boarders!" came another cry.

Billy heard it from his hammock in the forecastle, and still trembling, went up on deck to see a navy three-decker hove-to and lowering one of its longboats. Minutes later, a lieutenant stepped aboard.

"His Majesty's Ship, *Belipotent* requires men," he announced in a strong voice, then his eyes swept over the crew and lit on Billy Budd.

"I'll go," said the handsome sailor. And then he ran back to his hammock to collect his things, being careful to leave the captain's blue shirt and black hat behind.

"Ah," said the lieutenant, seeing Billy Budd return, and having dissuaded Captain Graveling's pleas, "Here he comes; and by Jove, lugging along his chest—Apollo with his portmanteau."

They descended to the longboat. Shandy Weaver came up on deck, nursing a swollen jaw. All of his crewmates lined the port rail. He joined them to see his handsome sailor being rowed over to a man o' war.

Ah but that, me lad, be a very different story.

King Ludwig's Dream Machine

Not all that long ago, tourist Tommy Warden could hardly wait for a chance to visit the fabled fairytale castle of Neuschwanstein. More than a century before, because it was his job, Hans Schmerzmann wearily inventoried the silly place. But just five years earlier than that, Christian Jank dreaded entering its haunted halls, and this despite the fact that he had designed the castle.

1999

"The best games are those that we play with ourselves," thought Tommy Warden, as he began the ascent to Neuschwanstein Castle. The fun part was that in private games only he knew the rules, and therefore could almost always win. Tommy's favorite private game of late was that of beating Bavarians to their goal. After all, they were so proud of their prowess in hiking and especially climbing. Young or old, heavy or thin, they were always forging ahead, forever laughing and all too often singing, and oh-so-sure that they would be the first to get there. Tommy, trim and very fit at the hearty age of twenty-six, was just the man to beat any German to the goal.

This day the wondrous goal hovered high above on a rocky crag, occasionally peeking down through the overhanging pine branches. "New Swan Stone" was the most romantic of medieval castles. Disney had copied it, and damn near everyone had seen its image on some old calendar. Funny thing—all of these everyones were in love with an elegant fake. Neuschwanstein had been built in the 1870's as a Victorian gothic extravaganza for Ludwig II, "The Mad King" of Bavaria. Reality can never be as good as a dream, especially mad dreams.

Tommy Warden, fledgling American architect, loved his first trip to Europe. He had enjoyed an entire summer of architectural wonders: Great Houses of England, Loire Chateaux, Italian villas, and now his real favorites —the follies of Ludwig II. He had also indulged his other passion: seducing, and/or yielding to, European men. It had been an "awesome" summer.

But the great game awaits. Ahead, just starting to hike up the steep winding road that led up to the castle, were two youngish Germans. Blond, of course, and so typically healthy—more—tight black lederhosen displayed firm cheeks and lithe thighs. The requisite knee socks bulged over robust calves. Good hiking boots promised big feet— Tommy liked that—and bleached linen shirts, with the sleeves snugly rolled up, showed off well-developed biceps, covered with that fine thin gauze of golden hair that is oh-so-very German. Oh yeah, these were the guys to beat to the top.

Tommy let them forge on toward the first curve. The great game might be a private one, but there were rules, and winning only had validity if the unknowing competitors had started with a definite advantage. Of course, Tommy would race with his own special handicap. A forty-pound knapsack was strapped across his wide shoulders.

The two Germans were beginning to be obscured by a host of other tourists who were charging up the serpentine road, but not before Tommy had noticed one other thing about his quarries. They really liked each other, laughed happily at common jokes, looked warmly at each other as they laughed, patted backs and waists—Oh yeah—they were probably "sisters." And therefore even more fun to beat to the top. "Here we go," said Tommy to himself, finally shoving off as the two happy hikers strode out of sight round the first bend.

Ludwig would have understood. His had been a life of private games. That's why Tommy liked to read about him. Ludwig had built the castle of Neuschwanstein and two other follies for his solo entertainments. And then there were all of those private performances of Richard Wagner's operas. Singers singing their hearts out to a dark theatre, not really sure whether the King was watching from his royal box. But he was. Tommy, from the vantage point of all his reading, was sure of this. And the tumultuous music of, say, *Tannhäuser*, must have swept the King into ecstasies, squirming with joy, downright orgasmic in the safe inky shadows of his gilded theatrical cage. Such expensive and exquisite private games! Tommy was jealous.

He strode forward, passing panting suburban Americans, insolently sauntering Frenchmen, the ever-chatting English, and not a few rushing Germans, none of whom knew that they were in a race. The omnipresent Japanese were striding well, but not well enough. Tommy turned the corner and saw his youthful German quarries ahead, laughing on their way up to the second dogleg of the road.

Closer now, the last of the Japanese falling by the wayside, Tommy could begin to hear his unknowing racers' conversation.

"Wahnsinnig? Nein, der König war nur exzentrisch," said the one on the left,

"Wie Du!"

"Wie Ich?" laughed the other, "Nein, eher wie Du, mein freund."

Tommy didn't care if they thought the King was mad. Ludwig had played his private games and almost won. The young architect chased their heels toward the last bend in the road, and prepared to win his own private game. The ideal challenge would be to pass right between them.

The next turn was some fifty yards ahead. It would lead to the red brick gatehouse of the castle. Tommy strode faster, straight as an arrow, cleaving his way through just as the two Germans were about to resume their conversation.

"Entschuldigen sie mich, bitte," he said, as he shouldered his way, but they parted only to keep abreast of him. This would not do. Tommy picked up the pace to an almost running stride—and, damn, they matched it!

"You are American, nein?" said one, racing on the left with plenty of breath in reserve.

"Yeah," said Tommy, with an even faster stride.

"And in a hurry, ja?" laughed the other, with a new burst of speed.

"Ja," answered Tommy, realizing that somehow this game was lost. He never should have charged down the middle. Damn.

"I am called Heinrich," said the one on the left, panting just a bit

"And I am Villy," added his friend, making a "W" into a "V," and panting too.

"Tommy," volunteered our architect, with a slowing sigh, as they approached the gate.

"Vell, Tomas, since you are so anxious to see this place, let us buy your ticket," said Heinrich, and "Tomas" demurred with a defeated thanks. His new friends bought the tickets and the three entered the lower courtyard of the castle.

"You like to hike, Tomas?" said Willy, with what was most definitely an appraising look.

"Yeah, a lot." Tommy answered, aware of new private games.

"You see that bridge floating in the mist?" said Heinrich, pointing up at the Marien Brücke, which spanned a gorge high above the castle. "Ve are hiking up there afterward for the best view of the castle. You vill join us, ja?" A too-familiar shoulder pat punctuated the question.

"Ja. Danke," said Tommy with an inviting smile.

"Gut," said his new friends in beaming unison.

They turned right to follow the crowd into the entrance hall of Neuschwanstein, where a uniformed guard at the door collected tickets. Then the whole hoard trudged up a flight of stone stairs to a long Romanesque corridor that led to 'Der Palas.' Here guides waited beneath signs of various languages.

"For you, ve take the English, ja?" said Willy. Warm back pat, of course.

"Sure," said Tommy, "Aber Ich verstehe Deutch."

"Ah, but you are our guest," said Heinrich, with his own warmer pat.

"Danke," said the twice patted, as they planted themselves in front of a sturdy middle-aged lady, whose blond (of course) hair was plaited in tight braids (of course) that wound round her head like a laurel wreath. She welcomed them to Neuschwanstein and introduced herself to the group as "Gertrud Schmidt." And of course she counted them.

"Twenty two. You must all stay together. We wouldn't want to lose you to the ghosts!" Big laugh, of course. And boom, she was off, recounting Ludwig's general history at break neck speed as the group raced after their leader down the gallery, passed through the formal entrance hall, and charged up the white marble spiral staircase of the North Tower.

The older Americans puffed behind. The English jabbered in the middle. Our trio led the pack. Gertrud halted at the first landing, backed by an archway leading to a long hall, which was blocked by a red velvet rope and a sign with the words 'Eintritt Verboten.' "Here You may not enter," said the guide, "but then there is nothing to see, only spaces in unfinished brick that were to be guest rooms for a King whose guests were only imaginary." Another laugh, of course.

Tommy wished he might have lingered behind. One of the joys of being a tourist is that you could decide when you understood a language. It would have been such fun to plead ignorance and jump over that rope. Then again he was hardly alone, flanked by his well-bronzed Germanic bookends. Ah well...onward and upward...

"Schnell, schnell," said Gertrud, "faster please," as she herded her flock from the rear.

"Tough cookie," thought Tommy, with chagrin.

The second landing was unobstructed, so that the flock spilled out into a wide medieval corridor of dark richness. "Funny," said Tomas, to his friends, "that so white a building could have such dark interiors."

"The better for Ludwig's dreams," said Heinrich, patting.

"And for his dream guests," added Willy, patting too, but a little lower. Tommy smiled.

Gertrud led them through the King's private suite: ante-chamber, study, living room, and even an imitation of a grotto—stalactites and all. In the gothic royal bedroom, Tommy was enchanted by the exquisite decorations. But his companions giggled, especially at the many murals of German chivalric legends, which glowed within the dark wood of richly carved frames.

"The ladies in these paintings are all so...Brunhildishe, Nein Villy?"

"Ja, Heinrich. But the knights are...how vould You say it, Tomas... hunky, ja?"

"Ja," said Tommy, beginning to weary a bit of them, and their pats.

Then the fair Gertrud led them across the corridor into the castle's grandest interior, the high domed "Tronsaal," with its dazzling columns of lapis lazuli topped by gleaming golden capitals. Ahs and oohs abounded. At the far end, steps led up to a gilded mosaic apse where the throne (never finished) would have been. In its place, on a golden easel, hung a life-sized portrait of the young King in a dashing blue uniform.

"Das ist unmöglich! Es ist Tomas," said Heinrich, with a gasp.

"Ya, it could be you, Tomas!" added Willy.

And an awestruck Tommy suddenly realized that they were right. So did the other tourists. Even Gertrud narrowed her eyes to focus on him.

"You see, I told you we had ghosts!" She said, garnering yet another hearty laugh from everyone but Tommy, who stared at his... reflection? Ludwig was tall, just like Tommy who, at six feet three inches, towered over his German companions. Both had a slender grace, though Ludwig's shoulders were not as broad and square. But it was the face that truly reflected. Long wavy black hair. Chiseled bones. And the dark piercing eyes. Tommy had met his doppelgänger.

"Come," said Gertrud, breaking the spell, "We must go up to see the Singer's Hall."

The two German's dutifully marched to her call. The others followed. Tommy stayed and stared. A moment later Gertrud appeared on the balcony above. "Come along 'Ludwig'," she cooed, "up the staircase to your left. Schnell, schnell."

Tommy shook his head, trying to end the trance, and ascended the marble stairs. But he didn't leave at the next landing—he didn't know why—he just kept spiraling up to the top.

And found there the most thrilling of Neuschwanstein's sights. Eight white marble columns reached up to an azure dome covered with golden stars. The central support of the spiral stairs became a soaring palm tree, whose white marble leaves knifed outward, radiating across the starry sky. The banister coiled around its base to metamorphose into a marble dragon covered with gleaming scales.

Tommy looked deeply at the dragon, ran his fingers over the lustrous surface. God, it felt grand to have left the others behind, especially the too-cloying Germans.

Then, looking into the dragon's mouth, he noticed something strange. One of the teeth had a very straight crack along its base. He reached out to touch it, and the tooth swung back on a hidden hinge. Tommy heard a quiet groaning from somewhere above. A panel had opened in the wall. Now this was fun!

He walked up the last step to the opening. Beyond was a narrow stone corridor. Of course he stepped through, and found another marble dragon's head mounted on the wall. It too had a cracked tooth. He touched it. The panel behind him swung shut with another groan, and utter blackness enveloped Tommy "Ludwig" Warden.

Gertrud, extolling the virtues of the remarkable Singer's Hall, had forgotten about the recalcitrant American tourist who so resembled the King. "Ah well," she thought, "he's probably still staring at *his* portrait." She showed her flock the remarkable chamber at the top of the spiral stairs, then herded them back down to the third floor lounge with its balcony over-looking the Tronsaal. She looked down. "Scheisse!" He wasn't there.

At the end of the tour, full of shame, she alerted the sweep guards that an American tourist named Tomas was still somewhere in the castle. They searched for an hour but could not find him.

Outside the gate, Heinrich and Willy watched and waited for their exciting new friend. After a while they gave up and began their hike up through the forest to the Mary bridge.

Tommy Warden didn't panic in the utter blackness. He fumbled in his knapsack for the trusty little flashlight, and finding it, proceeded down the twisting stone corridor. At the far end was a thick wooden door with huge iron hinges hammered in the shape of dragons. He pressed the thumb latch, and entered a large, pyramid shaped stone room, lit by an oculus high above. In the center of the chamber was the damnedest contraption that he had ever seen.

1886

"The trouble with suicides," thought Hans Schmerzman, "is that everyone else is left behind to clean up the mess." He sat in the deceased's chair, surrounded by every oil lamp that could be found, in order to provide some decent working light in the gloomy study of the Royal Dearly Departed. Directly behind him was a huge oak cabinet, carved in the gothic style. Here had been found the endless memoranda, inventories, and detailed architectural plans of the late King's follies. Other papers mounted upward in piles, looming over the huge desk like castle towers.

He stood, removed his Prince Albert coat, flung it over a chair, cleaned his pincenez, wiped his pronounced brow, and sighed, primly. "Prim" should have been his middle name. For six months he had pored over these documents, and climbed through the three castles to catalogue the effects of Ludwig II. Hans Schmerzmann, trained professional archeologist and would-be re-discoverer of the real past, had been assigned the grimy task of inventorying the creations of a mad suicide King.

Bavaria was rich with genuine artifacts of the Middle Ages. Why couldn't this spendthrift monarch have made his dream world by collecting those objects? Hans would have been proud to help his King in that more honest endeavor. But no, Ludwig had squandered his fortune on ersatz theatrical fakes from the workshops of Munich. There was simply no justice. And it was all the fault of that wastrel bohemian, Richard Wagner, who had doomed reality and dazzled the impressionable King with an avalanche of vulgar romantic operas. Scheisse!

Three very fat ledgers sat in the middle of the desk. They accounted for almost everything. Not only were the contents of the three castles listed, but also all of the uncompleted projects, like the half-gilded throne that sat in a Munich atelier. On top of the ledgers lay the last remaining mystery. Here were several bills of lading involving huge sums, dating from five years before, and for five utterly different kinds of work. But each was marked in Ludwig's hand with the mysterious words Freude Fühlen—"to feel the joy."

He had tried to contact the five artisans. One made mechanical organs, one did upholstery, and one was a maker of clocks and automatons. Yet another executed fine cabinetry and gilding. But the last was the strangest of all—a renowned puppeteer! And none of them could be reached.

The clock and organ makers had immigrated to America and left no forwarding addresses. The cabinetmaker had abandoned his lucrative trade to become a lowly ship's carpenter and was sailing somewhere on the other side of the world. The upholsterer had died of honest old age. And the maker of marionettes had been murdered in his shop. So Curious!

Yet the bills had been paid, and a delivery date of April 15, 1882 was clearly noted on each bill. The destination was Neuschwanstein. Curiouser and curioser.

There seemed only one way to get to the bottom of this, and that was to question those who had served the King. One last round of interviews and Hans would be free. Oh how he dreamed of joining his friend Heinrich Schliemann, who was doing such important work in Greece. He cleared away the papers and ledgers, and rang a bell for the first of the interviews.

"Otto Schwenk, stable boy," announced the guard stationed outside the door. A handsome blond lad entered and stood rigid at the far side of the desk.

"Sit, sit." said Hans. "You served the King during April of 1882?"

"Ya, mein Herr," answered the young man, sitting bolt upright.

"Did anything strange happen of the Fifteenth of that month?"

"I...I couldn't help it. I was new to his service. He made me. There was no choice."

"What do you mean, Herr Schwenk?"

"We had all been ordered to leave the castle that evening. Everyone who served the King. He stood there by the gate with his equerry, who checked our names off on a list. We were to stay away for six days. I was one of the last to leave. But the King stopped me and told me to wait in the room over the gatehouse.

"I went up the stairs and opened the door to a large dark chamber. All of the shutters had been closed. I found a chair by the wall and sat there in the darkness for a long, long time. All I could think of was that I had done something to anger the King. I had heard that he had boxed the ears of several other servants.

"Then a great rumbling sound came from the courtyard windows. I could tell that several wagons or coaches had arrived. I started to open one of the shutters, but heard the door creak behind me. There stood the King, a black silhouette towering in the opening. I sank to my knees and bowed, touching my head to the floor, in the manner that he demanded. He closed the door and then said 'You must remove your clothes now.'

"I thought surely that I would be whipped, but could not find the reason. 'Please, Your Majesty, what have I done to anger you?' But he simply said 'Strip off your clothes'." Otto faltered.

Hans saw his pince-nez begin to fog. This was not the interview that he had expected.

"And then, Herr Schwenk?"

"Then...then the King kissed me on the mouth...and more. Down my chest and...and...took me in his..." Young Otto started to cry.

"That's enough, Schwenk," said Hans, wiping his brow and handing the handkerchief to his guest. "You need say no more. I did not realize that our King had such...depraved proclivities. Catch your breath. And do not worry. I have taken no notes. My real interest is in regard to those wagons. What did you see of them?"

"Wh...when the king...finished with me, he said nothing. Just left the room by a different door. I dressed as fast as I could and ran to the bottom of the stairs. The equerry met me there. He gave me a bag of coins and this ring." Otto held out his hand to display a handsome ring set with diamonds in the shape of a fleur-de-lis. "He said I must never tell anyone of my 'rendezvous.' I didn't. I swear. Until now."

"I believe you. But what of the wagons?"

"Oh yes. I had forgot. The equerry pushed me out of the gate, but not before I could see that four large wagons and two coaches were drawn up in the courtyard. They weren't there when we returned a week later."

"Thank you, Herr Schwenk. You are excused."

"But I couldn't help..."

"Excused!"

Hans was despondent. None of the succeeding twelve interviews could furnish an explanation of what the mysterious wagons had delivered, but several of the servants had seen fit to blurt out their own stories of the King's decadent lust. Hans had tried to stop them. Oh to be pure and prim again! But it was as though each of the handsome young men needed to atone by telling their stories—and displaying their rings. The King's staff had been nothing but a sodomite's seraglio. Oh dear, this would not do.

And it did seem as though history was plotting against Hans, for several years ago he had made an important discovery in Rome—a wondrous silver hoard created for the Emperor Comodus—only to see it revealed as a terrible example of the perversion that dare not speak its name. The Vatican had confiscated the treasure as well as his report. Damn this seeming conspiracy of sodomites!

One last interview. And Please God let it provide an untainted answer. Hans rang the bell. Richard Hornig, the late King's equerry, was announced. He sat with dignity and composure.

"Good afternoon, Herr Hornig. I do not care to hear any more stories of the King's...personal relations. My only interest is to discover the nature of that which was delivered to this castle on April Fifteen, in the year 1882."

"I do not know, Herr Schmerzmann."

"Yet I have witnesses who can place you here on that day."

"No doubt they can," said Hornig, with unshakable aplomb, "but I left just after seeing Otto off. And then, at the King's command, I locked the gate, and went home for a week. I saw the wagons and coaches, but can tell you nothing of their passengers or contents."

"And who could?"

"Alas, only Lorenz Mayer, who was the King's most loyal valet."

"Summon him, please."

"I cannot. He disappeared on the night of the King's arrest. And no one has seen him since."

Richard Hornig was perfectly composed. But Hans Schmerzmann squirmed and perspired as though *he* was under investigation. He had to get to bottom of this. Hans placed the five invoices in front of the equerry.

"Herr Hornig, I have personally searched this castle from the lowest vault to the highest tower. What ever was delivered had to be of some size. What, and even more maddening, <u>where</u> could it be?

"I do not know. Two years later I left the service of the King. Yet several servants have told me the strange story of the King's last night in this castle, and the answer might be there. It seems, upon learning that he would soon be deposed that the King was desperate to have the key to the north tower. They kept it from him for fear that their Sovereign might jump to his death from the battlements. But I knew him well enough to be sure of his great fear of heights. It was a fear more strong than any desire for death. I think he may have wanted something else, and it was in that tower."

Hans concluded the interview and raced to the spiral stairs of the north tower. He scoured every stone, but could find nothing beyond the expected openings leading off the landings and up to the topmost lookout. The trained archeologist did not notice a crack in the dragon's tooth. Back in the King's study, he pored over the plans of the castle, but there seemed to be no possibility of another chamber.

Hans was defeated. His report would be prim enough to leave out the sordid tales of Ludwig's perversions. It would also say nothing of the five invoices, which even now had crinkled to ashes in the fireplace.

1881

Ah sweet dreams, so beautiful and clear at the moment of waking, only to evaporate with the first bite of breakfast. Twenty years earlier, in 1861, the King had offered Christian Jank the secret dream of every theatrical designer—the opportunity to create something that would last.

A scene painter makes his living by realizing wondrous dreams with insubstantial materials. Temples and royal barges, mountains and tempests, palaces and peasant huts—anything you want can be whisked up with wood and canvas and paint—and skill. But eventually, after the final performance, these painted dreams end up stacked in the alley, waiting for the wagon that will take them to the bonfire. All of that skill evaporates in smoke. Sad.

Yet the young Ludwig had used his eyes as well as his ears during all of those private command performances of Wagnerian operas. He had seen Christian Jank's visual skill in making dreams come true. Soon royal valets were delivering notes of praise to Jank's studio. Next came the ring with the diamond fleur-de-lis. And then the summons to an interview at the Royal Residenz in Munich.

Jank presented his invitation to the majordomo. A footman, dressed in livery of blue and gold was summoned to guide him to the King's presence. The two paraded up the grand staircase, through miles of state rooms to a spiral birdcage of gilded steps that led to the very top floor. Then down a corridor, stunning in its depiction of Wagnerian bombast, to the King's study.

Christian was dazzled, not by the sumptuous décor which was, well, very theatrical, but by the genuine beauty of the twenty-year-old King. No wonder every girl in Munich swooned at the thought of him. Even a scene painter twice the King's age found himself staring with impolite intensity.

"Herr Jank, how good of you to come," said the King with a clear, strong, youthful voice that matched his slender classical visage.

"How very gracious of Your Majesty to have invited me," answered the painter, with a deep bow.

"I have admired your work at the Residenz Theatre, and would discuss a project of my own."

"I should be much honored to assist Your Majesty."

"Splendid. Come see my new winter garden."

Then Ludwig led Christian through a tiny door into a vast crystal dream. A glass conservatory had been constructed on the roof of the palace. Palm trees and lush hillocks floated in ponds fed by fountains and waterfalls. Tiny Oriental pavilions dotted the landscape.

"How wonderfully Magic!" gushed Christian.

"Ah but it needs a vista, don't you think, Herr Jank? That far blank wall should present us with a view of the soaring Himalayas. Would you be so kind as to paint it for me?"

Thus began their dream collaboration. Two years afterward, the King invited Christian to spend a day at Hohenschwangau, the royal family's summer retreat in the foothills of the Bavarian Alps. Ludwig took the painter for a long carriage ride, and then an exhausting hike to a pile of Gothic ruins high atop a wondrous rocky crag. The King stood well back from the cliff edge, gesturing toward the lake far below, reciting lines from <u>Lohengrin</u>. Christian sketched furiously.

"We shall call it Newschwanstein," said Ludwig, standing like a god with the wind whipping through his black, wavy mane. "How soon can you furnish the final drawings?"

Back at his studio, Christian Jank drew and painted at a whirlwind tempo, for he had fallen in love with a King who would allow him to make a dream that might last through the ages. You must understand that this was only the deep platonic love that an artist often feels for his patron, for Christian's sexual fantasies were only of the ladies.

There followed years of drawing and painting. Three different castles were now abuilding, plus two more on the drawing table. Twenty years of re-drawing and re-painting. And hundreds—no, thousands of notes from the King. Change this. Redo that. At first so charming in their requests, but then over time, more demanding, more impatient, more scathing in their criticism. Through two decades the dream had changed by stormy degrees into a nightmare.

And so had the King.

Oh, Jank knew all of the gossip. The intense infatuation with Wagner, which was defeated by the composer's greed and the public's outrage. The disaster of a failed marriage engagement of the King and his cousin Sophie. The too-close friendships, first with a prince, and then a chevalier. Then the rumors of dalliances with mere stable boys. And now—God forbid—an amorous alliance with an actor! So very sad.

As his fortunes fell, so had the King's physiognomy; his belly bloated, face puffed, even his teeth lost to a love of sweets. Now the once dashing vision had become a repulsive recluse. And Jank dreaded the latest summons to Neuschwanstein.

He stepped off the train on an appropriately black and stormy night. Waiting to carry him was a black coach drawn by four black horses. And black was his mood during the journey up to the castle, which sometimes flashed ghostlike above in the lightning. The valet met him in the courtyard.

"Good evening, Herr Jank, if one can say that."

"Ja, if."

"His Majesty wishes to see you immediately."

"Tell me, Lorenz, what is his mood?"

"As stormy and black as the night, I'm sorry to say," whispered the valet as they ascended the marble stairs. "The incognito trip to Switzerland with the actor ended, as usual, in disaster. His Majesty paces all night and broods with imaginary friends. Come see me after your meeting, and I will have food and good strong drink for you. You'll need it. And I will better explain the King's latest...dream."

The valet led him through the dark ante-chamber and scratched, ever-so-lightly on the door to the King's study. A low, downright ghostly voice said "Enter." Mayer opened the door and Jank fell to his knees, bending forward to touch his head to the carpet, hating himself and the King for this ridiculous new royal requirement. Mayer closed the door. One small multi-colored oil lamp glowed in a far corner.

"Good evening, Herr Jank. You may rise," came a dark rumble from another darker corner.

"Thank you, Most Gracious and Exalted Majesty." Jank stood, and knew he would continue standing no matter how long the meeting lasted. The King hulked in the huge chair beside the desk, but it was impossible to see his face. Jank moved closer.

"NO, Herr Jank. Remain by the door."

"Of course, my King."

"The One True Friend once said that We had no ear for music."

"That cannot be true, Sire, for Your Majesty's love of Herr Wagner's, I mean the True Friend's, music is well known."

"The stories, Jank. Not the music. We will remedy that failing. We have decided to let you help Us to feel the Friend's music."

"But Sire, I am no musician, only a painter."

"True. Yet you can design anything...anything in the world. We have seen that on the stage and in Our castles. We have just come back from the land of William Tell, where We saw a remarkable mechanical orchestra.

"You will design such a device, Herr Yank. It will play the divine music of the True Friend, not only on the instruments of His scores, but also, through other, more sensual means, upon the human body—upon Our Body!"

Christian Yank was struck speechless.

"Of course, in this modern world of a crude and senseless public, complete secrecy must be maintained. My valet has all the details and will inform you. You are dismissed."

"But..."

"Dismissed!"

Lorenz Mayer waited in the outer corridor. He guided a shaken Chirstian Jank down three floors to the castle kitchen, and poured a good, stiff brandy.

"I feel older than my sixty years, Lorenz. Our King's dreams have given me too many gray hairs. But this latest nightmare will drive me to my grave. I must leave his service."

"I well know your meaning, Herr Jank. But you must not do that. I think his latest dream may save him."

"A depraved machine that 'plays upon the body.' How can that save anyone?"

"Our King's nightmare is that he loves men more than women, and he hates himself for this. Yet he cannot control his desires. Oh Herr Jank, you should see his secret diary. Every time that he touches a man is listed as a 'Fall,' and followed by sacred oaths that this will be the last.

"I read the diary during the day when Our King sleeps, and it breaks my heart, Herr Jank. But then, the next night, he will look out of the window, see a handsome stable boy, and ask me once again to be his procurer. It tears my spirit apart, Herr Jank."

Christian drained his glass and the valet poured another.

"We both have loved our King, Herr Jank, but not in *that way*. And we are lucky, being—beg your pardon—not so handsome. You make his dreams and I serve him. Now, perhaps only we can save him. For no handsome man or beautiful boy can meet Our King's conflicting needs. All of them, from Prince Paul to the actor Kainz have been unable to find that balance between loving intimacy and royal respect that he demands. And so, disaster. But this machine? It could serve by being a new kind of dream."

"Verdammte, Lorenz!" said Jank, draining his glass again. "Why don't you just 'procure' a music box and a masseuse?"

"A masseuse is still a living, breathing man, Herr Yank. It would not work." He poured two glasses and half downed his own.

"But I can't even begin to think of how to design such an infernal machine!"

"Oh of course you can. Think of those mechanical orchestras. Springs and cogs and levers and bellows play the instruments. Mix in some extra linkages, and they could be like keys that 'play upon the body'."

"Ya, I suppose. I begin to see it. Another, please."

The valet poured two more glasses of the King's cognac.

"I am no artist, Herr Jank, but might I suggest a linkage between sound and sensation? Perhaps feathers for the violins, puffs of air for the woodwinds, something scratchy for the horns, for the drums something that strikes the skin, and for the cymbals—ah, perhaps that's a lashing thing!"

"Ja, ja, I can see it now," said a very tipsy Christian, "and I cannot believe that I might create the nightmare which is in my mind's eye."

1999

Tommy Warden was ever methodical. The first mystery to be solved was one of location. He thought about the curving, then zig-zagging stone corridor, and realized that the pyramid chamber must be right over the throne room. That would make it, if viewed from the inner rafters of the roof, seem to be only a reinforcement for the dome below. And therefore perhaps this was a secret place that had never been visited since Ludwig's time. God, this was fun!

Then he considered the contraption. What ever it was, was now gray beneath a century-old layer of dust. He walked around it. The back was a mass of complex machinery. At one side several winches could be turned to raise a series of counterweights. But the front—ah, there was the grand mystery.

Deeply carved gold molding framed a circle, perhaps eight feet in diameter. All around the outside were musical instruments that seemed more real than carved. Inside the circle was what looked like a vertical bed, covered with padded deep-blue velour. So strange. But there was much more.

Tommy rummaged through his knapsack for an old sweatshirt, which he used to flog some of the dust away, coughing in his new-formed cloud of grayness. A famous image emerged. Embroidered in gold in the center of the velour was a life-size version of Leonardo Da Vinci's drawing of a nude man, legs together and arms straight out to describe a perfect square—then, from the same figure, legs and arms splayed diagonally to inscribe a circle. And at the ends of the splayed limbs were gold devices: below, two shelves shaped for feet and above, two strong handles. Very strange, but weirdest of all, was the figure's face. It wasn't that of Leonardo's Vitruvian man, but the face of young Ludwig—and therefore Tommy's own likeness.

Then, as he dusted more, Tommy saw the horde of ivory hands. Perhaps three dozen of them reached inward from the edge of the frame. Some held feathers, some tiny bellows, some small wheels of leather chips, some bits of fleece, still others held whips. This was weird and downright sexy. At the very bottom of the frame two other hands held what looked like a large gilded fig leaf. Really sexy! And all of the ivory hands were mounted on little brass tracks, which led to the embroidered outline of Leonardo's Ludwig-Tommy. Oh boy!

At the left side was what appeared to be a control panel. Tommy dusted, and revealed labels. The dial marked "Laut-Ruhig" (Loud-Quiet) was balanced by another equally calibrated dial labeled "Stark-Weich" (Hard-Soft). Then there was a long line of toggle levers, each linked with one of Wagner's operas. Oh boy, oh boy!

The natural light, beaming down from the oculus above, had begun to fade. Then Tommy noticed the oil lamps hanging from points in the ceiling. And, yes, they still held fuel. He rummaged again in his knapsack for matches, found them, and gloried in the romantic flickering light of a century past.

He began by winding up each of the counterweights. And was astounded by a blast of music. Tommy ran to the control panel and turned off the toggle marked Die Walküre. Of course, that must have been one of Ludwig's favorites. Ah, good. Safe silence again. Luckily for Tommy, all of the night guards were three stories below, enjoying Schnapps and a noisy dinner in the royal kitchen. No one had heard the ghostly rumbles.

Methodical. That's the key. Tommy took his knapsack off to a corner to consider what he had learned. He removed some bread and cheese that were to have been his lunches for the next few days, and uncorked his treasure—a bottle of Piesporter Glaubtröpfschen Spätlesse, '97.

So—he had discovered Ludwig's greatest private game, his sex toy to end all sex toys—a device which could play upon the King's body in direct relation to the soaring sensual music of Richard Wagner. Oh boy, oh boy, oh boy! This was really, in every classic sense of the word—Awesome.

Tommy took a last swig of the delicious wine. The time had come to commune with Ludwig. He removed his clothes, stood there facing the machine, and felt himself swelling below in awesome expectancy.

But always method. First things first. He went over to the control panel, and turned the dial to quiet. No sense in creating curiosity on the part of guards. The second dial was set halfway between strong and soft. Good. This had to have been Ludwig's setting. Tommy would go with it. Oh God was his erection expectant. The Walküre was a fine choice too. A thrilling one, in fact.

He flipped the toggle on, backed up the steps of the frame, placed his feet on the golden shelves, and took hold of the gilded handles. Then he felt the cool night air on his body, looked down to see his skin shimmering in the flickering light, and felt his stiff penis arching straight up toward the crest of the pyramid.

First, there was a whirring sound. Then the ivory hands reached up and out from the edges of the frame and started to move towards Tommy's body. He could see that little brass tabs preceded them on the tracks and, by gosh, stopped each hand at what must be the proper distance needed for its effect. Clever, these Germans. The only hands that did not advance were those directly below, the ones that held the fig leaf.

Then the Walküre music began. Strings going "Zarum, zarum zarum"— and with them eight hands bearing feathers that twirled, lightly stroking his arms and legs and sides. Not tickling at all. Not funny either, but somehow pleading, and oh-so sensuous.

Then the brass—trumpets announcing the famous theme—"Bah-bup-bah-ba-bahh-bah!" Eight more hands held little wheels, each with three tabs that could whirl out. One side of a tab was covered with fleece. These now bent inward to stroke, or rather, knead his sides. Pleasant. But then the theme darkened and deepened with tubas, euphoniums and French horns. Now the little wheels reversed so that the leather side of their straps slapped, stinging his arms and thighs and sides. Yet this too was strangely pleasurable.

Next came that part where armor-plated sopranos would have sung "Ho-jo-to-wo," but flutes and clarinets did the job. And were accompanied by the hands bearing small bellows. Little puffs of air wafted his flanks, and there was the faint hit of perfume. Oh course. Ludwig would have loved that! But there also had to have been other bellows blowing into tubes hidden in the blue velour. For when the echoes sang, puffs spread between his toes and through fingers and past the sides of his neck. THIS tickled!

Now the Brass theme came back with a vengeance, nipping giggles in the bud, blaring, slapping, stinging, making his skin glow hot and red, reaching for a crescendo that made him scream out with his own song. Then falling notes of strings, and feathers relaxing, calming, stroking. And Tommy, burnished with sweat, heaving with relief, reveling in the cooling puffs of air that marked a frenzied dialogue of flute and clarinets.

Next an oboe played the first of the Valkyrie laughs, and Tommy laughed too, for it was accompanied by a blast of air right up his ass. Ah German humor. The "voices" sang now in counterpoint with the famous theme, and a still laughing Tommy played Elmer Fudd, and laughing more, added "Kill the wabbit!"

But laughing died when the theme came back in its fullest force. The brass wheels slapped in rapid pace, yet there was more. Every bar led off with a cymbal crash and that meant that the last six hands, each with whips of multiple ends snapped forward to flail his pecs and abs and thighs. These were wild thrashing strokes that stung with insane mounting vengeance. He held tightly to the handles, and screamed without any thought of method.

And then Tommy looked down to see that the fig leaf was rising. Its interior was lined with what seemed to be waving fur. God this was scary —and wonderful, he thought—just before the fig leaf clamped over his penis. Then thought was abandoned.

Every single hand was hard at work, stroking, slapping, whipping. Ho-jo-tee-whas blew past every part of his body, and whipped his long black hair straight out in front, lashing his face. And below...Oh below... pullulating fur tugged at his balls, rippled up his cock, seemed to suck and stroke and sting, sparing only the tip, which strained and stabbed to stay clear of the gilded leaf. He sang out with the Walküries—"Oh Wagner, oh Ludwig, oh God!" And then the long crashing crescendo chord—and semen shooting straight up, a torrent of it, spattering his chest and neck and face. And at last, the dying away of music in fevered descending strings, the sinking of the fig leaf to the frame, and forced Valkyrie laughs which somehow echoed the rivulets of sweat and pearly white juice that dripped down across his heaving chest.

Tommy let go of the handles, and with wobbly legs, retreated to collapse by his knapsack and the lovely bottle of Piesporter.

Two floors below, Horst Brüchner, who had fallen into his usual Schnapps sleep on the floor of the King's bed room, woke with a start. Where was that music coming from? He tidied his uniform and lumbered out into the corridor. Louder now. He could feel it rumbling in the walls and floor. Horst entered the throne room. Up there? But then it stopped. He went back to the bedroom and reached under the King's bed for his hidden bottle. Dreams, that's all, dreams. Sleep, that's good, sleep.

High above, Tommy was ready for more. He re-wound the counterweights and scanned the control panel. Ah yes—<u>Der Fleigender Hollander</u>. Oh yeah, Tommy would happily fly with that Dutchman.

One story below, Horst was out cold.

The next morning, Tommy Warden waited in the dark corridor, hearing a French speaking tour guide describe the wonders of the dragon and the palm tree. A moment after she and her flock had left he opened the secret panel, re-shut it using the dragon's tooth, caught the rest of the tour, and sauntered out of Neuschwanstein. He would never return. Thereafter he was known to spend many evenings listening to the music of Wagner. But he would never again be able to sing "Kill the Wabbit."

The Ballad of Sadie

She trembles in supplication before the great chief. He sits in state in front of his tee pee, looking supremely stern, as is his wont. The young girl clutches at her budding bosom and inches her way forward with a hard lump of fear in her throat. He lets the dry hint of a smile flash across his sun-weathered face. She halts, wide-eyed. He looks on through lids that seem lizard-hooded. She reaches out, still trembling, to tender her humble offering. He leans forward, accepts it, raises his sharp point, and then...well then Chief Sitting Bull signs the autograph, hands the program back, and gestures to the red bucket at his side. The girl fumbles through the pocket of her pretty white-lace summer dress for a nickel, drops it in, curtsies, and flees.

"Greetings Great Chief, having a good day are we?" chirped a bespectacled man with an oversized handlebar mustache. Sitting Bull, being the proverbial Indian of very few words, simply reached down, hefted the pail, and shrugged. The dapper visitor withdrew a watch from his brocaded vest, while the chief gave him a long, hard once-over.

"Ned Buntline, when you come to town?"

Ned smiled, having bet his self that it would take a full thirty seconds before the Great Silent One would make an utterance, and he was right.

"Just today. Got a new set of stories for Bill to take a look at."

"But you not write about me."

"Nope. I respect your wishes, Chief."

"Good."

"Besides, I figure that I'd have to wait and listen continuously through far too many moons just to get you to tell me enough for a five page piece. Ain't worth it."

"Mmm. Better."

"Want to amble over to Bill's tent with me? By now he'll have happily decided that the sun has sunk below the yardarm."

"Mmm, maritime anachronism...Sure."

July in Philadelphia can be every bit as hot and dry as any western plain, even at sunset. Ned and the Chief shuffled through the dust, raising a minor cloud of it on their way through the back lot of the Wild West Show and Congress of Rough Riders. The day's performance was over. They skirted a line of wooden stakes as they passed the long horse tent. They skirted horse droppings too.

Annie Oakley's tent had achieved the illusion of a little oasis. A platoon of well-watered pots provided a surprising garden. Real flowers competed with the floral drapes of her canvas cottage. The drapes won. Annie, who was also signing autographs, waved from her porch as they passed. Then she blew a kiss to the Chief, whose stolid face cracked into a warm smile. He even blew a kiss back. Sitting Bull loved that little lady, and she returned the compliment.

The next tent, the big one striped with red, white and blue, was 'Colonel' William F. Cody's. And just to make everyone doubly certain of that, high over the awning flapped a large canvas version of the famous poster—a charging buffalo, bearing an oval portrait of Buffalo Bill in all his silvered tonsorial majesty. Beneath was the motto "I AM COMING!" A clink of glasses and the deep rumble of laughter emanating from within the patriotic pavilion assured everyone that He had indeed come to Philadelphia. It was also apparent that the sun had plunged below Bill's yardarm some time ago. Ever the gentleman, Ned held the canvas flap back for the chief, and they entered Colonel Cody's canvas castle.

"Why damned if it isn't Bull and Buntline come to imbibe my Bourbon! Welcome Gents."

They returned the Great Scout's greeting while the Bourbon was poured, and not in those little civilized glasses. No, sir, these were mighty large tumblers. Greetings were also exchanged with the two other drinkers present: Nate Salisbury, who managed the show, and sharp-shooter Frank Butler. They all raised a toast to what was left of the real Wild West, and then the host turned to his newest guest.

"Ned, what brings you to the City of Brotherly Love?"

"Stories of your boyhood, Bill. Just finished. Thought you might like to peruse them before the public does."

"Oh goody, I get to find out what my youth was like, though I doubt if my memory could ever grow as tall as your tales."

"Now, now, Bill, I'll bet you'll find these to be, well, mostly true."

"Oh, don't matter much. You and me have grown rich with these dime books of yours."

"They do help to sell tickets," added Salisbury.

"I'll drink to that!" Said the Colonel, and he did, as did the others. "So you tell 'em tall, Ned, tell 'em all tall"

"Hell, Colonel, you'll drink to anything," said Frank Butler, as he took his own gulp.

Sitting Bull said nothing and sipped. Everyone was silent for a while.

"Ned," said Cody of a strange sudden, "did you ever hear a tale that was too tall to tell?"

"Nope, can't think of one, Bill. Barnum was pretty right about suckers."

"Never heard a tale you...couldn't tell?"

"Well now, <u>that's</u> a different kind'a thing. There's tales can get you sued, on account of they're insulting lies. Then there's tales that are state secrets, and telling those might get you clapped in jail. Though I can't say if I ever heard one of them, seeing as I don't hobnob with presidents and such like you do, Bill.

"I'll drink to that!" boomed Butler.

"You keep it up and tomorrow Miss Oakley will outshoot you again," said Salisbury.

Butler decided to join the Chief in sipping.

"Damn, Ned," said Buffalo Bill, while stroking his white goatee, "I just thought it might be fun to hear a tale that shouldn't or even couldn't be told."

"Oh I might be able to scare up one of them for you. See, there's a bunch of tales that can't be told. For instance, there's tales of tail."

"You mean..."

"I do, Bill, and even more forbidden than those are the tales of...er... strange love. I could never print them. Of course in Paris you can get all kinds of wild and wicked stuff."

"I wanna hear a tale that can't be told, Ned." It seemed that Cody was in his cups, just a mite. "An' I wanna hear it now." Ned decided to compose himself to tell a tale, for it could prove troublesome to deny the Colonel when he was thus.

"Good thing, Miss Oakley didn't join us tonight," said Frank Butler.

"Mmm." said Sitting Bull.

Nate Salisbury drew up a chair. So did they all.

Ned Buntline took a long thoughtful drink from his own tumbler, paced a bit, twirled his mustache for a while, and then turned to face his audience.

"OK, I've a tale in mind. But first I'm gonna ask some questions. Bill, you and I spent lots of time out West, and we've known many a cowboy, right?"

"Right you are, Ned."

"And how many of 'em was Negroes?"

"Oh a few...maybe."

"A few? More than that, Bill, in fact, damn near a quarter of 'em."

"Nah, that many?"

"You bet your boots, Mr. Buffalo Bill."

"Well, come to think of it you might be right. There were a lot of black faces out there."

"Mmm, Ned is right," nodded Sitting Bull.

"OK, Colonel, how many negroes do you have performing in the show?"

"Why, none, Ned. Got plenty workin' in the back lot though. And we're good to each and every one of 'em. Right, Nate?"

"Right you are, Sir."

"That's not the point, Bill!" said Ned with a fervor that surprised them all.

"Then what is the fuckin' point, Ned?"

"That Negroes are a part of the cowboy story...a pretty sizable part... but damned if I can write about them, or if you can show them in your show, because we're both in the business of creating an American legend and none of our fellow Americans wants to hear that a part of their sacred legend might have had black faces. Now, damn it Bill, <u>that</u> is a tale that can't be told!"

Well, there was a considerable quietness for a while...but it was a drinking silence.

"You ready for another question, Bill?"

"Don't rightly know that I am, Ned."

"Well, get ready."

"OK, shoot."

"Weren't too many of the ladies out West, was there?"

"Now damn it Ned, if you're gonna try to tell me that there was a lot a cow girls, I'm..."

"Hold your horses. I got something else in sight."

"Can't wait to hear it."

"The few ladies...er, women that we knew out there were pretty damn expensive. Right?

"Yeah, I guess."

"And the cows weren't a very good substitute."

"Oh good God in Heaven, I begin to see where you're headin', Ned. You're gonna tell us that all of them cowboys was a bunch of buggerin' bastards!"

"No, not all, Bill, not by a long shot, but maybe a lot more than you'd care to admit."

"Aw Jesus, Ned, why'd ya hafta..."

"Cause you asked me for a story that <u>couldn't</u> be told, and damn it yourself, that subject is just about the Goddamndest couldn't-est that there ever was."

"Oh hell, pour me another, Nate. Fuck, pour us all one."

Nate got up to pour, and the Colonel, being both high and dejected, as well as down-right rude at times like this, took over Nate's chair for a foot rest

"Go ahead, Mr. Buntline. Tell yer damn tale. An' it better be a good one. Got one of yer fancy titles?"

"Yup, this story's got everything we just talked about...all of it...and I'm gonna call it... "A Tad Too Complicated"

I learned this tale in an old run-down saloon plunked out on the edge of Abilene, Kansas. Walked in on a hot, dusty afternoon not unlike we had today. Nobody was at the bar when I took my stool. There was only a cowboy sitting at a table way back in the shadows. Weren't no bartender in sight neither. So I sat a while and twiddled my thumbs. Thought I heard the sound of sniffing maybe, then I knew it was weeping, and turned back and realized that it was the guy back in the corner. Then I looked harder and saw that he was a Negro. Well, that's it, thinks I, I've done wandered into a saloon on the wrong side of town. So I got up to leave when all of a sudden a white lady comes bustlin' out of the back room and pops up right in front of me.

"Well hello Mister, what'll it be?"

"I dunno," says I, "maybe I'm in the wrong place."

"Why's that?"

"Well…" says I, with a quiet nod to the back corner.

"Mister, we serve any and all. You bothered by that?"

"Why no. I just didn't want to fall afoul of…"

"Well don't you worry none. Now what'll it be?"

So I ordered a whiskey for myself, and just to make things better all around, one for the man in the corner. He thanked me, raised his glass, then sank back into shadows and sniffling. And, well, you know me, I'm a curious critter. Always wanna know the why of things, because that's the manure that can help a good story to bloom.

"What's wrong with him?" Says I to the lady bartender, who I realize is kinda pretty in a no nonsense way, meaning she won't take no nonsense from nobody.

"What do ya mean?"

"Well, he's awful sad, isn't he?"

"So am I, we're both sort of in mournin'."

"For who?"

"For the man we love."

I think I choked a bit on my whisky. "Your father perhaps?"

"Nope."

"Bother?"

"No, an' not an old uncle, neither."

"Well, Hell, you can't mean…"

"But I do. I surely do."

"But you said 'We,' and well, you're a…and the cowboy's a…and who was…?"

"The Love we're mourning is the handsomest, most wonderful, most bravest cowboy you ever could know. He's tall an' blond an' gorgeous. His name is Thaddeus P. Lovejoy. 'Course, we both call him Tad."

"I'm a tad confused," said I, but she wasn't amused. "Aren't you mixing your tenses? I mean how can you mourn someone who 'Is'?"

"Oh Tad ain't dead. He's just gone forever."

"No hope of ever coming back?"

"Nope, none."

"How can you be so certain of that?"

"Cause we both know him an' love him an'…well, now we know he's gone off to a better place."

"So then he IS dead!"

"No, he ain't! He's as alive as you an' me. It's just that he's gone off to what he thinks is a better place. His earthly Heaven so to speak"

"Well then, why don't you just up and follow him?"

"Cause he doesn't want us. Leastwise that's what he said."

"Maybe," I whispered, "he doesn't want <u>one</u> of you."

"I feel bad sayin' it, but I wish that could be true. 'Course so does Jacob."

"That the cowboy in the corner?"

"Yup. Tad don't want neither of us."

"But how do you know that?"

"Because he wrote us a letter."

"Can I have another drink, as well as a couple of more questions? Hell, make it one more for the cowboy and one for yourself." I flipped three dimes on the bar.

"Thanks, Mister. Shoot."

"This question might be a tad more—oh, sorry—a bit more personal."

"S'OK. Ask." She refilled my glass.

"Did you both love him at the same time? Sort of together-like?"

"Of course not. Wadya think we are? A couple o' perverts?"

"Well, no, I…ah…just thought…that maybe…"

But she was off to the cowboy's table with his drink.

"Jacob thanks you," she said, sitting beside me at the bar. "We both made love with Tad in our separate places an' times an' ways. It's just now that he's gone, we're consolin' each other."

"You weren't...well...just a tiny bit jealous of each other?"

"Course we were, something fierce, 'cause we were both sure that the other one was Sadie."

Now this was getting to be a tad too complicated, even for a story teller like for me.

"Damned if I ain't afraid to ask..."

"We were too. Ya see when ever Tad pleasured me...an' believe me he knew how to pleasure...why when we got to the...well, you know...the... pinnacle of pleasure...well, then Tad would scream out 'Sadie, oh Sadie!' over and over. And since my name is Cassie, you can understand that I might be a little disconcerted-like."

"Understandable, indeed."

"Well, this went on for about a year. Tad an' Jacob would ride into town when ever they had finished a drive and was flush. And sure enough, there'd be that smilin' handsome face at the bar round closin' time with a bouquet of wild flowers that he'd picked for me, an' we'd tip toe up to my chamber. That was followed by the heaven of his body and then, damn it, the hell of hearin' 'Sadie, oh Sadie, my Sadie.' "

"Didn't you ever ask him about..."

"Well, sure I did. Many times. But all he'd say was 'Sorry,' an' nuthin' more. So then I noticed that he always came to town with his nigger friend— sorry, Jacob—just slipped out."

"No matter Cassie, I got other things to think about," said Jacob as he drained his glass. I slipped a quarter onto the bar, and Cassie brought the remains of the bottle over to his table.

"At any rate, I soon noticed that when ever Tad was pleasuring me, Jacob would spend the night waiting out front with the horses. And I thought that's strange, because there are dark gals here in Abilene to please men like Jacob. So why the hell would good lookin' black fella like him wait all night out front?"

"Why, indeed?"

"Well, jealousy is a nasty worm, an' nuthin' nurtures it better than hearin' a different girl's name screamed out at the pinnacle of pleasure. So I started askin' questions. Found out that Tad an' Jacob lived together in a little cabin 'bout ten miles north towards Buckeye. So then I started watchin' 'em when they came into town. An' pretty soon I could see the love in Jacob's eyes every time that they walked in. Never could quite make it out in Tad's manner though, but as I said, jealousy doesn't help anyone see straight. 'Sides, we all heard tales of men who secretly take on women's ways, an' I was getting' pretty certain that 'Sadie' might be Jacob."

"But it weren't." Said Jacob with a little kind of wail, and sunk his head in his arms. Cassie crossed over and patted his shoulder.

"I know Baby, and I'm sorry. Ya know, Mister, here we are pourin' out our hearts to you, an' we don't even know your name."

"Ned. And I'll buy another bottle."

"Comin' up, Ned. What you doin' in these parts?"

"Well, I'm not sure I should tell you, not at least if I want to hear the rest of your story."

"Why's that?"

"Because I write dime novels and such. And that seems to make lots of people think twice before they tell me something."

"Ah, for fear you'll tell it to the world."

"Exactly."

"Ain't no fear of that, Ned. Not with this story. First nobody would believe it. Second, well, there's some things you just can't write about without getting in a heap of trouble."

"Such as?"

"OK, Jacob," said Cassie with a wicked smile, "Now its your turn."

"Lordy, I don't think I can."

"Sure ya can, honey. This new bottle of whiskey says ya can. Come on over. Tell him your side, and just to make it easier I'll leave you two alone, and go of upstairs to find the letter and that other thing to show Ned." Cassie bustled off. Jacob came over to the bar.

"Mr. Ned, you sure you wanna hear my part of the story?"

"Well, Jacob, maybe not all of it."

"Most important thing is I loved him."

"I can see that. Eyes are a pretty good window to the soul."

"Thing is he pleasured her, and I jes' loved pleasuring him."

"I got the picture. Don't need the details. But I bet the same thing happened. You brung him to pleasure and he yelled out the name of Sadie."

"Yessuh, ev'ry time."

"Drove you crazy."

"Did, Suh. An' at first I thought Sadie was the White Man's nickname fer Cassie."

"Not that I know of."

"No, Mr. Ned, it weren't. I learnt that when Tad started goin' for his night-time rides."

"To see Cassie?"

"Nosuh. He said he was goin' off for a ride with Sadie."

"Aha, now we get to meet the mysterious lady!"

"No, Mr. Ned, we don't. Fact is, the mystery gets worse. Some nights, 'bout sunset, Tad takes his leave, saddles up his horse and rides off to the woods west of our cabin. He comes back maybe two hours later. Says he been off with Sadie, an' sluffs off to bed. Well that ain't 'nuf time to get to Abilene an' back, so I knows it ain't Cassie he's seein'."

"So I'll bet you tried to follow him."

"Yessuh, I did think of it. But that's a hard thing to do in a flat place like Kansas. 'Cept fer that clump of woods 'bout a mile off, ain't nuthin' else clear to the horizon. Man can see a nuther man for miles. Ain't easy, nosuh, not easy at all."

"Well, how'd you do it?"

"Didn't. I jes borrowed me a telescope, waited til a bright moon night when Tad had rode off, an' I climbs up on our roof with that telescope. Well, I sees him ride into one side of the woods, then a couple a minutes later he rides out the other side and gallops outa sight to the west. An' here's the weird thing. He galloped away nekid. 'Cept fer his hat and boots, weren't not one stick o' clothes on that White Man's hide. Well, I never seen him come back from meetin' Sadie, cause damn it all, I fell'd asleep up there. Much later I hear'd him trotting back an' had jes enuf time to skedaddle down from the roof an' crawl into my bed."

"So the elusive Sadie was still a mystery."

"Yessuh, she was."

Cassie came back with an envelope and some papers.

"OK Ned, I guess its time for the Day-noo-ment. See, Mr. Writer, I read some too."

"I am impressed, Cassie."

"Good, ya should be. So four weeks ago Tad up and disappears. Jacob, here, lets a week go by, an' then decides to stop in here an' see if I know where Tad's gone."

"Hell, Cassie, I was hopin' he was here."

"I know, Jacob Honey, but we both know he weren't. Well, that was when we two decided that misery loves company, to say nuthin' of good wiskey. Besides, I could use a good helper, 'specially on Friday nights, and so Jacob moved in the back room here."

"Sides, Mr. Ned, weren't nuthin' to do but wait an' hope," added the cowboy.

"Well we only had to wait another week, an' that's when this letter came."

Cassie handed me the envelope and papers.

"Ned, you gotta read this one first."

It wasn't a very long letter, but the penmanship was surprisingly neat.

"Read it out loud, Ned. Jacob can't read but he likes to hear it. An' I guess that's why Tad sent his letter to me, but addressed it to both of us. Go ahead. Read."

So I did.

"Dear Cassie and Jacob:

I'm mighty sorry to leave you both this way, but about a week ago I met a fellow in town who told me about a remarkable thing, a kind of place I've always dreamed of. And he offered me a job learning his trade. So that's where I am. You both have been very good to me, but I'm here and you're there and it's got to stay that way. Sorry.

Yours truly, Thaddeus P. Lovejoy"

The other piece of paper was a hand-written poem

The Ballad of Sadie

Sweet Sadie reclined on her blanket,
A warm golden glow on her skin.
She said "won't you ride me,
'I want you astride me.

Oh cowboy, that can't be a sin."

Sweet Sadie could spread my legs better
Than any man ever could know.
I'd mount her and grab her,
So damn glad I had her,
She felt wondrous jist lyin' below.

Sweet Sadie would quiver beneath me.
I'd hug her with both of my knees.
I'd bind myself to her,
An' strive to subdue her.
Oh Sadie, my Sadie, oh please!

An' then we'd ride off when the sun set,
Both glowin' and nekid and free,
Racing fast 'cross the prairie,
'Cause that horse would not tarry,
While carryin' Sadie an' me.

Sweet Sadie an' me in the moonlight,
Would race cross the plains in a breeze.
Oh Lord, how I'd squeeze her.
And stroke her and tease her.
Oh squeeze back, my Sadie, oh please!

My horse would leap high over sagebrush,
An' then I would tense up and cheer:
"Sweet Heaven," I'm screamin',
"Oh God, now I'm creamin',
On Sadie, my saddle so dear."

You boys can all fuck yer pink ladies,
Yer cows, or yer sidekicks. That's fine.
But to Heaven I'll ride,
With my saddle as bride,

Jist lovin' that Sadie o' mine.

Then I looked at the envelope. The rubber-stamped return address said:

Sam Stagg

Fine Saddles and Leather Work

Miles City, Montana

"Well, that's it. And maybe it was 'A Tad Too Complicated.' Cassie and Jacob were both hugging each other and crying up a storm, so I left a gold dollar on the bar and said my good nights. Haven't told that story to anyone but you gents."

Buffalo Bill snored.

"Boy, I'm glad Annie didn't come," said Frank Butler.

"Mmm," nodded Sitting Bull.

Nate put an arm on Buntline's shoulder.

"Ned, I've some friends in New York who would pay damn well for stories like..."

"Nope. That one stays outa print. Good night Gentlemen."

Sitting Bull left too. The moon was out and it was cooler.

"Good story Ned. But glad you not print it."

"You're right chief. So am I"

Sitting Bull lit up when he saw Annie Oakley was still sitting on her porch.

"Night, Ned." He shuffled off to sit with her.

"Night, Chief."

Ned Buntline took the late train to New York.

Shiva's Smile

Harry hated India. 'Leftenant' Harry Harden-Payne loathed the place, which suffered only two kinds of weather: 'dry as dust' or 'monsoon mud.' Harry couldn't abide the food. "Can't curry my favor—what, what?" Most of all, Harry despised the people. Damn blighters gave genuine meaning to the expressions 'teeming hoard' and 'great unwashed.' They were all such bloody ignorant blokes with their stupid, round-hipped, many-armed gods and all of those idiotic sacred bulls. Their ashen skin color wasn't pigment, Harry thought. Oh no. It was naught but dirt, universal dirt, eons of dirt.

And as for the wildlife? Well, Bucko, don't bother with those tigers or cobras. There were worse things—far worse—such as the infernal omnipresent bugs: vast armies of gnats and mosquitos, troops of beetles, and most frightening of all to Harry's mind, huge spiders. Bloody awful place, India.

And what did Harry like? Oh regimental duty of course. That goes without saying. That, at least, was English. Beyond which, Harry had a passion for two things. One was wrapped in an oilskin packet that he kept in the sabertache hanging from his scabbard. The packet contained a collection of several diamonds, two small rubies, a most respectable emerald, and a string of unmatched pearls. This was his nest egg. Ill-gotten, of course. A little gaming here, a little cheating there, to say nothing of the strange disappearance of a little Hindoo pawn broker.

But if Harry had to bear this God-forsaken place, then by God there ought to be something better someday back in England—the possibility perhaps of a nice little farm somewhere in Shropshire, and of a nice little stable with some nice big stable boys. This was Harry's prime passion. Ah, young men, especially the stable boys and farm hands of good old England.

He had so enjoyed being an upper-level boy in public school days, administering the cane to taut, pink, brawny asses. *Brawny* was Harry's favorite word. He had loved the way those fair-skinned, round-armed school boys had of wincing, stiffening, and holding back tears. But Harry would always get them in the end. "Got that? In the end—what, what?"

His passion had been hampered here in India. As an officer he could, and did, order punishments. Then the triangle would be set up, and he could watch the Cat o' Nine redden a sunburned private's brawny (Oh, lovely word) back. But the sergeant had all the fun. A lieutenant could only watch from a respectable, regulated, most unsatisfying distance. And besides, you couldn't trump up too many charges without destroying morale.

No, Harry's needs would have to be managed in other, more private ways, which depended on the one good thing about living in the midst of teeming hoards. Life was cheap. Boys could be bought.

Indian boys weren't Shropshire lads. Never could be. "You can't make good English Stilton from bad goat's milk—what, what?" No hardy, clean-scrubbed, pink-white, brawny bodies here. No, sir. If Indian boys weren't round flabby lumps, then they were skinny, stringy ones. Especially the *untouchables*. Shropshire lads were born, not made. But Harry could try. By God, he would try.

To this determined end, Harry, who as an officer was not required to live in the barracks, had rented his own digs—a small bungalow on the edge of the English enclave. Oh it had all the requisite features: reception room, veranda, and a high surrounding wall. But what the Lieutenant liked best was the little two-stall stable and carriage barn at the back. Chestnut, his stallion, got the stable. The barn was for the boys. It had thick wooden beams, no windows, and plenty of room to hang what Harry called his "grooming tools." These included several riding crops, leg and hand irons, a well-worn cat, razors, a lathering cup, and, of course, a good stout strop or two. And rope. Lots of rope. White cotton, not hemp, because the former looked better on ash gray skin.

Though untouchables might be uncouth pagan louts, nonetheless they had a kind of wisdom in the way of the streets. They could be wary, but they were always hungry. That was their most useful weakness. Harry could hire houseboys for no more than a rupee a week. He'd order them to comb his horse, and clean out the stable muck. They'd make mistakes. He'd see to it that they did. Harry would harry them (What, what?) until they did something wrong, because then he could administer punishment. Indian boys were good for only two things—beating and buggering.

One was out there now, last night's entertainment, manacled to a beam, probably sleeping on the hay-covered floor. But he had been no substitute for a Shropshire lad. They never were. Scrawny, not brawny. Harry had shaved every inch of him as he was bound to the beam. You had to. Such hairy little brutes. Yet you could never call the boy clean scrubbed. He had flicked his crop and strapped his strop over every inch of that body. But where was the victim's bravery that made it all worthwhile?

These boys didn't hold back tears. They just bloody screamed like banshees. No stiff upper lip. No stiff anything for that matter. Later, when Harry had impaled the boy on his saber— not the metal one, but the fleshy one between Harry's legs—that hadn't been stiff either.

Oh how Harry hated India.

But enough of morning musings. Time to get up and out. Duty calls. Harry pushed aside the mosquito netting, swung out of bed and stretched, admiring himself in the large pier mirror that he had brought from good old England. He was brawny indeed; good strong thighs that filled out jodhpurs right proper; well-formed chest that might pop the buttons on any dolman; nice round arms that could swing a saber; and clear pink flesh without any hint of a tan. But then Harry always wore his full uniform during the day, no matter how hot it got. "Mad dogs and Englishmen—Ay what?" And clean scrubbed? Indeed yes. Harry shaved himself every day from face to shins. Harry, at thirty two, was still a Shropshire lad, and he would bloody well remain one.

Shaved, uniformed, booted and sabered, he stepped out onto the veranda, and down to the well, drew up a pail of water, opened the carriage barn, doused the boy, undid his manacles, and watched the little bugger snatch up his loincloth to run off and rejoin the underbelly of the teeming hoard. Then Lieutenant Harry Harden-Payne mounted Chestnut and rode off into the sunrise to find proper civilization in the form of a hearty English breakfast at the officer's mess.

Three weeks and five houseboys later, Harry still hated India.

One evening, while returning from a regimental review, he galloped Chestnut through the crowded streets on the way to his bungalow and reined in at the gate, almost running down some stupid, orange cloaked monk who stood nearby. Dismounting to unlock, Harry looked back to see the bald young man sprawled in the gutter, reaching out to gather the—what?—seeds?—that had spilled from his begging bowl.

"Bloody bugger better not beggar me," Harry muttered. And then, for the first time, India seemed to whisper in his ear.

The orange cloak was fastened over one shoulder, revealing an arm that wasn't exactly scrawny or brawny. Lithe was the word. Neither ashen nor white, it was golden. And most wonderful of all, that arm was hairless, smooth, silky—like young Stilton, golden ivory Stilton. The monk, or priest, or whatever he was, rose with humble grace and stepped toward the lieutenant. His high-cheekboned face was hairless too, not even eyebrows, only long lashes that framed his downcast eyes. He held out the bowl, but when Harry surprised himself by reaching for a rupee, the young man surprised the lieutenant by offering the bowl's contents to the horse. Then, as Harry held open the gate, the monk led Chestnut down the drive to the stable door. Harry had trouble thinking. India was humming to him.

Grasping the handle of his saber, Harry hurried to open the stable door. The lieutenant drew his sword as the monk led the horse in, and placed its sharp point in the small of the young man's back. No reaction. No words. The monk simply tied Chestnut's reins to the stall and then stood there, facing away, waiting.

But Harry had words. In a husky whisper he recited a favorite little barracks poem:

"How glorious the saber, with its smooth and graceful curves,
Too perfect for the purpose it so bloody well serves,
For it's nothing but a cleaver that can chop a man in half,
As the Hussar charges on with a cheer and a laugh."

With a sinister little laugh of his own, Harry raised the blade to the side of the monk's neck, took hold of his arm, and guided him through the connecting door of the carriage barn. Then the lieutenant used his free hand to choose a set of cuffs, snapping them on the young man's wrists. Still no sound. The monk just stood there, head lowered, eyes closed, waiting. Harry reached up to a rope which dangled from a crossbeam pulley, closed its snap on the handcuff chain, walked over to the tie-off, and pulled until the monk's arms were raised so high that only the balls of his feet touched the floor. And India began to buzz.

Now Harry could think. The sunlight was fading. He lit several lanterns, closed the stable doors, and sat for a moment on a pile of feed bags. And then he walked up to his new victim and undid the shoulder clasp of the orange cloak. As it fell away, Harry quietly gasped. The young monk's body glowed in the lamp light: golden, chisled, clean-scrubbed, and completely hairless. No chest hair, no arm or leg hair, not even pubic hair, only the long, almost feminine lashes on closed lids. No expression. No sound except for rhythmic breathing. Harry heard nothing but the thumping of his own heart as he took off his gloves, unbuttoned his dolman, and removed his shirt. No buzzing flies, no humming mosquitoes, no chirping crickets. Even India seemed to hold its breath.

But not its heat. Harry could feel a thin sheen of perspiration glazing his chest. He could almost hear the sweat, savoring the silence as he stared at the monk's stretched body. And then the soft, barely audible sound of the tip of his riding crop caressing the well-carved planes of the young man's chest. Harry began, oh so slowly, so gently, drawing the crop along the contours of the suspended form, outlining the flanks, sketching the thighs, tracing the buttocks, the cleft of the back, the nape of the neck, and the smooth golden skin. It was almost like the sound of a pencil on paper, drawing a dream.

And then the tapping. Harry began to flick the crop. Stinging, faster now, with little slaps that matched the tattoo beat of his own heart. Down the lovely curve of the back, twitching between the legs, teasing the limp, uncircumcised cock, tapping up the lithe belly to sting the tits, and then taunting under the chin. Did Harry see stiffness there, in the long well sculpted cords of the neck? The monk's eyes were still closed, not tight shut, just closed. Waiting? Daring? This boy was indeed different.

Next the hiss of air, and the sharp answering thwack as leather belt met buttocks, leaving a welt not of red but rich amber, a rosy orange glow in the flickering lamp light. But still no sound from the monk, not even a gasp. More hissing thwacks as Harry watched the growing amber glow, almost weaving a pattern across the young man's back and rump, spreading the lustrous glow round his legs, painting him, making him—oh yes—brawny.

Now Harry wanted to hear something, a gasp of surprise perhaps, or even better, a scream. Better yet—pleading. Please. Harry needed to hear his victim's voice. He took up chains from the beams on either side and locked them to the monk's ankles, pulling his legs apart. And then a new sound like wind rushing through leaves and the sharp snare drum roll of Harry's cat stinging the boy's back. Did he hear a sharp intake of breath? Again. Was there a gasp? Once more. A low moan—oh yes—now Harry was happy. He was even more full of joy when he saw the young man's face, for there on the high cheek bones were tears, spread like jewels on the golden skin. Like school days. Ah, India bloody sparkled! School days.

Harry reached out as in a dream, to touch the amber welts, to feel the firm inner curve of the monk's neck, then the hardness of his nipples, the ripples of his abdomen, smoothness of inner thighs, the warming fullness of his penis, and most wondrous of all, the absolute silkiness of a young man's scrotum. He was certain that those oh-so-even breaths were forced, and that those eyes darted behind closed lids. Now Harry needed to hear his victim's voice.

His left hand reached down to his own organ, freeing it, stroking it. His other hand grasped the hilt of the cavalry saber, raising the tip to the monk's cheek, laying its blunt edge on a shoulder, all the while hearing in his inner ear the voice of an old headmaster mumbling something about the ceremony of knighthood—Arthur and Lancelot. Harry pulled the sword back, to draw its point across the throat, so lightly, not cutting, merely grazing, drawing a thin red line down the chest to circle one nipple and then the other. He saw, in his mind's eye, the old headmaster tracing a line on a map of Alexander's invasion of India, and heard the name 'Hephaesteon.'

The lieutenant stepped back to draw the line round the monk's flanks, over the shoulder blade, and down the valley of the back to the cheeks. He moved the blade forward between the young man's legs. Stroking slowly, forward and back, in and out. And again, memories of the headmaster, murmuring lectures of Christopher Marlowe and his play about Edward and... Gaveston. Then Harry remembered something else, the second verse of that barracks poem. In his best regimental manner he recited:

> "How shining is the saber and its sharp point too,
> Though it's nothing but a spike
> We've made to skewer you.
> And the Hussar charges on to the next Hindoo."

Harry kicked one of the burlap feed bags over behind the boy's legs. He drew the saber back so that its point just rested on the opening of the monk's anus, and then lowered the hilt to rest on the feed bag. Now his victim's eyes were open! Intense black pupils searched the lieutenant's face as Harry stepped back to the pulley tie-off. He took hold of the line.

"Please, Sahib."

Harry froze. The voice was low, even.

"It is my dharma to give pleasure to men. If I must die on your sword then so be it. But there are other, greater pleasures. Pleasures that can be yours, Sahib."

Harry's hands left the rope.

"I am called Bashwi. I am the last of my order. I serve a god whose image rests in a temple hidden in the jungle, a half-day's journey to the north. Once in each season I must clean my god's image in the perscribed manner, using only the tools on my body. If you would permit it, Sahib, I will clean your body in the same way."

Entranced like a cobra at the market, Harry removed the sword, the chains, and the handcuffs, while India whispered words from the Kama Sutra. Harry could only nod.

The monk guided the lieutenant to sit upon the pile of feed bags and removed his boots and jodhpurs, to begin in the strangest manner. He leaned forward, and with his tongue, seemed to lick a circle on Harry's forehead.

"Like some Hindoo mark," Harry hazily thought. Bashwi began with the toes, licking, sucking each one, and caressing with his lips the instep of one foot and then the other. Now Harry banished thought. Warm damp pleasure lapped his legs, the teased his thighs. And when Bashwi engulfed the Sahib's balls, Harry was incapable of thought. Soft silky lips, hot damp breath, and probing tongue seemed to swallow his whole being. The lieutenant thrashed, gasped, moaned with mindless pleasure, sinking into the pile of feed bags, feeling them transform into velvet cushions.

Now his penis truly was a sabre, arching up, oh so hard, rigid tempered steel, and yet so very tender. And Bashwi's tongue polished, honed, sharpened it to unendurable perfection. At last, the monk's mouth sheathed the fleshy sword in hot, moist, unbearable Heaven. India sang a thundering chorus, and Harry swam in a jeweled firmament on the very edge of explosion, when Bashwi withdrew, leaving his host heaving, gasping, breathless, writhing on a maharaja's bed of silken cushions. Suddenly, Bashwi was over him, licking once again that strange circle on Harry's forehead. And then, with serpentine grace, the young man reared back to impale himself on Harry's fleshy saber.

Words could never describe the lieutenant's ecstasy as the monk raised and lowered himself, squeezed and released, demanded and gave with hidden muscles. Sensations poured from Harry's every pore. Bashwi's hands were everywhere, like some six-armed Hindoo god, stroking Harry's sides, tongue lapping his chest, teeth stinging his nipples, lips brushing his neck. They played a raw duet of gasping throats, heaving lungs, beating hearts, and pumping secretions. Blood, sweat, saliva—and churning from deep inside, the throbbing, time-stopping rush, deafening roar, blinding white eruption of juices, and as they both shot forth, Harry's strangled voice rasping: "Oh lad, oh God, oh please lad, God, lad, please God, oh my brawny lad, Oh—My—God!

But with release came no rest. Harry felt the monk's tongue and lips upon his still throbbing cock, licking it, cleaning it, moving up across his chest, and lapping the burning trail of Bashwi's semen, which spread to Harry's neck. And then the boy brushed his lips over the lieutenant's cheeks, ran his tongue over the closed eye lids, and finally licked that mysterious spot in the middle of the Sahib's forehead. Harry dimly tried to imagine that spot, but India hummed a lullaby of deep sleep, and both succumbed, sinking side by side, entwined among the velvet cushions.

Early the next morning, as India's birds chirped *Reveille*, the two men stretched out on burlap feed bags. Consciousness returned to Harry. And questions.

"Is the Sahib pleased?" Bashwi murmured.

"Oh yes lad, yes indeed," Harry answered, "But I wish to know one thing."

"Yes. Anything, Sahib."

Then what, lad, were you doing with your tongue in the middle of my forehead?"

"Ah, Sahib, that is the place of my god's third eye. It is the all-seeing eye. The first and last thing that I must touch. The eye is carved from a great glowing stone of deepest red."

Now another voice began whispering in Harry's ear. It was the greedy voice of his other passion. And it urged caution, for Bashwi was describing a huge ruby, worth a veritable fortune—one that could ensure Harry a most happy and profitable retirement in Good Old England.

Tell me more about your god, lad." (Be careful, Harry.)

"He is called Shiva, Sahib. He is the god of fertility and ultimate destruction."

"And does he have six arms?" (Go easy, Harry.)

"Yes, Sahib."

"How big is his image?" (Not too fast, Harry.)

"Oh, nearly twice the size of a man, Sahib."

"I would like very much to see your god, lad." (That ruby is huge, Harry.)

"Of course, Sahib, I will take you to see him."

(The sooner the better, Harry.) "Now?"

If you desire it, then let it be so, Sahib."

This was too easy, too easy indeed, thought Harry, as the monk helped him regain his jodhpurs and boots. He invited Bashwi into the bungalow. (Don't let him out of your sight, the voice said.) With great speed, bantering while the young man looked out the window, Harry filled his knapsack with a lantern, matches, a crowbar, and of course, his pistol. Then, with Bashwi's help, he changed into a new uniform, locked up the house, filled his canteen at the well, saddled Chestnut, mounted him, and pulling up the monk from behind, cantered off again into the sunrise. This time away from civilization toward the verdant jungle. Towards Harry's wondrous ruby and the six waiting arms of Bashwi's god.

They left Chestnut in the care of an inn keeper at the jungle's edge, for there was no longer a road, not even a path. Harry had to use his saber as a machete. Bashwi, however, seemed to swim between the leaves, being careful to see that his sahib might follow—so careful that Harry forgot distrust.

Only once was their progress halted, when the lieutenant stumbled into a huge web with a terrifying spider that caused him to scream and Bashwi to return, finding his sahib pale, rooted, immobilized in terror. If ever the monk wanted to escape, this would have been the time. Instead he took the lieutenant's hand and led him round to a safer path. Later, when the heavy humidity changed to a blinding downpour—for this was the season of the monsoons—Bashwi trudged forward with Harry holding his robe. Even greed sang a sweet song of trust.

In India the deluge stops as abruptly as it starts. One moment you find yourself shrouded in impenetrable sheets of water, and then, so suddenly, like a curtain in the theatre, it lifts. Light now streamed through rising mist. Harry and Bashwi stood on the bank of a swelling river. Beyond, floating on an island in the middle of the rushing, muddy water, rose an exotic stage set. Golden, moss-covered sandstone walls supported the pinnacled dome of a great stupa. Carvings of elephants and sinuous cobras shimmered in the strangling shadows of huge vines, which climbed to the topmost spike.

And when a delighted Harry turned back—Bashwi was gone. (Now you've done it Harry. That's what trust will get you.) He would have to swim for it. (Hurry, Harry, before the litle bugger comes back with his friends.) There was no other way. He removed his boots and dolman, stuffing them into the knapsack, took off his saber, and carrying all overhead, strode into the rushing water. Harry was, thank God, a powerful swimmer. He had to be one in these swirling waters.

Halfway across, the lieutenant felt soft, slimy things seem to slide across his chest and feet. River grasses? And then, to his horror, Harry knew they were leeches, now slithering up the inside of his jodhpurs. He swam as fast as possible, while holding aloft the knapsack and sword with one arm, and paddling with the other, thrashing, desperate to stand upon the island.

Harry ran out of the water, stopping at the temple steps, stripping off his tight, waterlogged pants and gaped with disgust at the repulsive sight of long black leaches gorging themselves on his chest, legs, and even his groin. In a fevered panic he rummaged through his knapsack, found the matches, and one by one, burned the sickening creatures into release. Still queasy, he sat there in the sun, naked on the sandstone steps, trying to calm himself. (It's all right Harry, but you must hurry. Get that ruby. Now! Before Bashwi returns with the others.) Leaving his clothes to dry on the steps, Harry took up his sack, pushed aside the dense curtain of vines, and entered the temple.

Of course it was dark, but at least it was cool. Two lines of squat, bulbous columns supported a long row of heavy arches, like being in the belly of some monstrous whale. But at the rear, dappled by the light from unseen windows, was the shining statue of Shiva. Six bronze arms shimmered, almost waved, in the dancing light. And even from the doorway, some fifty yards away, Harry could make out the glowing third eye. It was indeed a huge and wondrous ruby—the biggest he had ever known, dwarfing the one that he had seen on the Queen's crown in the Tower of London.

Harry forgot the leeches, was oblivious to his nakedness, didn't even think about Bashwi and his friends, seeing only the great ruby. As he was drawn down the hall, he heard the scurrying of rats. It didn't matter. He noticed piles of human bones on each side between the columns and did not care. But when Harry finally stood at the base of Shiva's pedestal, he froze.

Stretched across the space between the six arms was an immense spider web. Its builder was nowhere to be seen, but the size of it made Harry shudder. Directly in front of the statue was a huge ivory spike, carved in the shape of entwined cobra tails, echoing Shiva's phallus, which curved up along the statue's belly. And high above, the dark bronze head of the god frowned, glaring outward with two pearl eyes and the all-seeing ruby.

Harry put down his sack, removing only the crowbar. (Work fast lad, you have very little time!) He squirmed between the ivory spike and Shiva's belly, and using the legs and arms as rungs, began to climb, pressing himself against the bronze chest, wanting above all to avoid contact with the awful web at his back. Higher, closer to his glowing goal, sweat streamed from his pores, streaking the idol's dark patina, oiling it, making his ascent so slippery. The lieutenant placed both of his feet on the giant folded legs, still pressing his chest to the god, rising slowly, crowbar ready in his left hand, nose grazing the rough patina of Shiva's neck, rising oh-so-slowly, past the chin, staring up, transfixed by the rich red fire of the ruby. Almost his. And then Harry looked into Shiva's scowling face. There, inches from his eyes, crouching in the contorted mouth, ready to leap, was the monstrous builder of the web.

In mute terror, Harry heaved himself back, turning as he leapt back into the terrible web, realizing that it was wrapping around him, his feet sliding off of the statue's legs, throwing up his arms, screaming. Howling, falling— hearing a click—caught, suspended. (Oh, my God!) Held by Shiva's hands. When Harry ceased screaming he heard a whirring sound, then the rumbling of some hidden mechanism. His feet had slipped into the constricting coils of the ivory cobras. His wrists were clasped by two metal hands. Two others cupped his chest. And the remaining two pressed upon his thighs.

Harry was feverishly trying to wriggle out of Shiva's grasp, when the ivory spike entered his bowel. His mouth gaped. No scream now. Just an empty, strangled rasp as the spike sliced into his entrails, as his head snapped back, and his eyes fixed upon Shiva's giant ruby. And the god's six hands pushed inexorably down.

Harry felt the snakes' tails seem to uncoil, slithering inside his belly, and then the jewels. A topaz fire spreading through his torso. Rubies throbbing through his veins. And from his testicles: pearls, growing, pulsing, pushing, rushing, shooting out of his penis, arcing out into the temple, looping in long strings across the stone floor. Then the diamonds: cold, hard, ice-blue, racing in from his extremities as he sank, followed by the deep black velvet of a casket's lining. Harry knew a jeweled joy, so much joy that he didn't care about the spider that had crawled around his neck and down to gnaw on his left nipple. Nor did Harry hear the scratching sound of hundreds of tiny claws as hungry rats followed the strings of pearls that led to Shiva's pedestal.

Several weeks later, when the monsoons had ended, there was a flash of orange in the clearing. Bashwi stepped out of the jungle, drew his coracle out from its cover of elephant leaves, and paddled across to the island. He gathered up the uniform and saber lying on the steps, pushed aside the curtain of vines, and entered the temple. Bones littered the base of the ivory spike, which threaded up through a bleached pelvis and ribcage. And perched on its point was Harry's skull. Bashwi gathered the bones and placed them with others in one of the niches between the columns. Then, in the prescribed manner, using only the tools of his body, the monk cleaned his god's image.

When he was done, Bashwi reached into the base of the pedestal to wind and reset the mechanism. For he had arranged, in a few weeks time, the visit of a young maharaja, lulled by Bashwi's body and drawn by the wonder of Shiva's third eye. His duties completed, the monk walked back to the temple gate, and turned back to see his god, shining in the dancing light.

And Shiva seemed to smile.

The Boy on the Red Velvet Swing

We must begin on the day when a shocking headline on the first page of <u>The New York Times</u> shattered the enviable perfection of Junius Pieter Morton's life with the unimaginable prospect of even greater perfection.

It was, of course, a predictably perfect June morning. J.P's valet had drawn the bath to just the right temperature of 92.5 degrees Fahrenheit. The towels were fully fluffed, razor well stropped, lather frothed, brush and pomade set out as prescribed, and mirror so carefully warmed that it would not dare to fog. Quite perfect.

J. P. emerged from his toilette to find hose, trousers, shirt and morning jacket laid crisp upon the new-made bed, and his black pumps polished to a lustrous sheen. Jenkins, the properly transparent valet, assisted in the robing, then tied the ascot with regulation panache, leaving to his master that which should be the only worrisome decision of a well-ordered day—the choice of a stick pin.

Surely not one of the diamonds. Too tony. Nor an emerald. Too flashy. On the other hand, a garnet might be perceived as a touch too sinister.

"Ah, One of the sapphires, I think. But no, not the blue, Jenkins— the purplish one, for there would seem to be just a hint of lavender in this cravat."

"Of course, Sir. An inspired choice."

"Quite exhausting, nonetheless."

"My sympathies, Sir."

A slightly weary J.P. descended to his morning room.

Here the catalogue of perfection continued. Sunlight streamed through Belgian lace curtains allowing soft shadows of Gramercy Park foliage to dance across the damask of the tablecloth. As was always the case, Beverly, the downstairs maid, had laid the table beautifully. Daffodils smiled from a cut glass vase. Goram silver guarded a Spode platter to display an edible flower whose pollinated center consisted of three Long Island eggs scrambled with shards of Maine lobster, which were set out upon twelve radiating petals of buttered rye toast points, lightly dusted with cinnamon. Cold jus de l'orange Valencienne and steaming Café Columbiana performed properly aromatic sentry duty.

Junius Pieter Morton flipped his tails and Jenkins slid a timely chair beneath the temporarily hovering derrière. The valet then withdrew to confer with Evelyn, the upstairs maid, regarding the laying out of day clothes. Back downstairs, J.P. shook out a linen napkin, downed the juice, sniffed the coffee, creamed it to the favored shade of fawn, and then chose one of four forks to prepare for the ultimate drama of depolinating his breakfast flower.

It was at this moment of morning exertion that the butler brought in a salver, upon which rested the most recent calling cards, the latest correspondence, and a freshly ironed, in fact still warm, copy of the Times, dated June 27, 1906.

"Thank you, Burton, and my compliments to Alphonse."

"Most welcome, Sir, and the chef will be quite gratified."

"I will need the automobile today, Burton. Would you be so kind as to have O'Reily bring it round at noon? I shall lunch at the club."

"Of course, Sir. And if I may be so bold, Sir, which club?"

"Montebanks. I think. Players, being just across the park, is depressingly close."

"Very good, Sir," said the butler as he bowed and took his exit.

J.P's right hand now floated over The New York Times.

But before hearing of the fateful moment when the newspaper was unfolded, let us consider a few of the remaining elements of perfection in

Junius Pieter Morton's life. To begin, he was twenty-nine years old, that happy age just before the last bloom of youth is sullied by any encroachment of wisdom. Second, his late English father—hence both the Junius and the Morton—having garnered a huge American fortune in railroads, steel and coal—had displayed the happy foresight to bequeath it entire to his only son. And he left it in such a way that J.P. had only the onerous duty of clipping bond coupons in order to reap millions. Though one did have to be careful to avoid scissors blisters such as might mar one's hands. Third, his Knickerbocker mother—hence the Pieter—had joined Father in languishing beyond the pearly gates. This additional passing had two distinct advantages. Firstly, no one was left to hound J.P. in terms of marriage, and lastly, it had occurred three years ago this very morning, which meant that today marked the end of formal mourning, thus the lovely and liberating mauve of his morning jacket.

There was one final crowning glory of his life. No women nattered within it. Oh from time to time some emergent social butterfly might have to perch upon his arm as the ticket of entrée for such as Mrs. Stuyvesant Fish's cotillions. But by and large J.P. could live in a state of blissful misogyny. That was one lovely aspect of the four men's clubs to which he belonged. Women never nattered there. They simply weren't allowed.

Ah, but what of Beverly and Evelyn, you ask? Then know that these two were English, and in that benighted country such names might easily be of the masculine gender, as in fact, in this case, they were. Not that "Bev" and "Ev," while gaily whisking through their work, didn't enjoy gamboling about in the aprons and starched caps that have always made maids maids. But when the door chimes sounded and respectability made an unexpected entrance, the two could quickly retreat to the accepted livery of footmen.

And now it was time for the Times.

J.P's right hand descended to take up, while his left ascended to unfold, and the paper demurely displayed its always sedate headlines.

ROOSEVELT RIDES RHINO. "What, again?"

KAISER CHARMS ALICE LONGWORTH ON YACHT. "I'll bet."

CORNEL SKULLS PAST SYRACUSE. "Ho, hum."

ARCHITECT STANFORD WHITE KILLED. "Oh dear, that cannot be!"

But J.P. read on and it was. Dear Stanny, who lived at the other end of this very block, and who had decorated this very morning room. Dear Stanny, who had housed the wealthy, designed their places of business, sheltered their prominent congregations, and brightened the streets of New York with so many edifying edifices. Dear Stanford had been shot dead by a jealous husband, while enjoying the opening of a show at the roof garden theatre of his own Madison Square Garden!

J.P. pinged the little silver bell.

"You rang, Sir?"

"I did indeed, Burton. Our Stanny's been shot to death."

"Oh dear, Sir. When?

"Last night."

"My most sincere condolences, Sir."

"Thank you, Burton. Now please let Jenkins know that we're back to mourning."

"Of course, Sir. He will be so disappointed. So will Ev. And just when color was about to bloom again." Burton left, head shaking sadly, leaving to his master the regrettable chore of delving more deeply.

That weird Harry K. Thaw, a lowly sewing machine heir, had done it. Which was doubly strange because everyone knew that Stanny had deflowered Evelyn Nesbitt several years before at his secret hideaway in the tower of The Madison Square Garden. Thaw should have realized that one couldn't return damaged goods after knowingly acquiring them. Oh dear, dear, dear. Poor Stanny. But that's what comes from womanizing: jealousy, recrimination, and unfathomable passion. J.P. would stick to men, who offered a modicum of logic and a dollop of licentiousness. That was incipient wisdom.

And now to change back into the awful garb and wend one's black, black way to Montebanks, which, by the way, the dear departed had designed. At least this particular period of mourning would not have to last three years.

––––––––

The minute that the electric auto had rounded the Thirtieth Street corner of Fifth Avenue, J.P. knew that Montebanks knew. The two bronze figures of Pierot and Pierette, which Gus St. Gaudins had sculpted to flank Stanford's spendidly rusticated arch, both held black crepe bows. Two others hung from the bronze doorknockers. A bevy of workmen were hanging more crepe swags from the balustrade of the Palladian smoking balcony above the entrance. Four stories above, the frieze of dancing Comedia figures seemed for today to trudge through the shadows of a deeply carved cornice.

O'Reily pulled over, and shot 'round to the curb to open the rear door. J.P. stepped down only to ascend the entrance steps and press the discrete button.

"Ah, Mr. Morton," said the doorman. "A sad day 'tis Sir."

"Sad indeed, Thomas."

Thomas took the black silk hat and walking stick, and J.P. headed for the burgundy and gold of the reading room. Only three members were present. Each had sunk into the womb of a wing chair facing a fireplace that Stanny had ripped away from some Loire chateau. None took any notice of J.P. who asked the barman for a pre-lunch Courvoisier, then ensconced himself in a window-facing womb from which eavesdropping was easy.

"Ah, but have you ever seen the infamous tower rooms?" Said the very recognizable voice of Joseph Duveen, antiquarian par excellence.

"Certainement," said James Hazen Hyde, Francophile par excellence, "I have attended several of his little contretemps."

"The bit about the red velvet swing," said the third man, some new actor by the name of Mansfield, "Miss Nesbitt and others swinging nude, is it true?"

"Of course," droned Duveen, "The seventh floor apartment is not large in terms of floor space, but the salon ceiling is quite high, some twenty-five feet I would surmise. The swing hangs there. But even more remarkable is the room with the mirrored bed."

"And did you notice the little toggle switches in the headboard?" Said Hyde, "Each controls a different set of colored lights. Quelle Romantique!"

"Pity," said Duveen. "I talked to McKim this morning. All is to be sold and disbursed. Stanford owed a fortune. Owed me too much to say."

Into every man's life there comes, at least once, a moment when one must risk all. J.P. had met that moment. You see, there was one tiny element of imperfection that marred his existence and that was Gramercy Park itself. Oh, not that New York's only private park wasn't perfectly lovely—of course it was—a leafy oasis languishing in the midst of a boring desert of brownstones. But even though the only keys to its gates were the exclusive property of the owners of the homes that over-looked the square, the park was still too public. That was the problem. Far too much over-looking went on. How was a young man to entertain other young men if the privileged neighbors continually minded more than their own Astors? Young women were difficult enough to smuggle in past the ever-prying eyes of local matrons. That was why dear Stanny (whom you will remember lived on the edge of this very park) had designed his tower hideaway. Anonymity is a product best found within a very crowded precinct, and at The Madison Square Garden anyone might turn down the wrong corridor and happen, quite unobserved, upon the new Otis elevator that ascended though the Garden's landmark tower.

Oh poor dear Stanny, you were so brilliant! J.P. Morton decided to clip a few more coupons and pounce.

Perhaps too many coupons had been clipped, but the wondrous key now inhabited the right breast pocket of J. P's vest. The electric auto be damned. J. P. would perambulate to his new triumph. He sauntered west on Twenty-Third, and swung north for the short walk up Park Avenue. During his initial exploration of the property, J.P. had entered through the public lobbies of the Garden. This time he would try to find the little private entrance around the corner on Twenty-Sixth Street.

"Why all these crowds at the ridiculously early hour of noon?" thought J. P. as the tower loomed above. He shouldered his way through a knot of not-too-elegant children and found himself face to face with an elephant. Oh of course, Barnum and Bailey were making their grand entrée, and the hoipalloi were assembled in hopes of hoopla. How very inconvenient, to say nothing of gauche, to have the prospect of circuses playing directly beneath one's secret pleasure dome.

J.P., upon seeing the crowd that crammed the sidewalk, surmised that the only way to get past to his doorway was to...oh dear...to join the parade? So he boldly strode forth to accompany the last of twenty-eight elephants, and that was when he looked up to see, ensconced in a jeweled howdah atop the animal's hump, the most exquisite of Ganymedes. A young man of spectacular form, stunningly revealed by spangled tights and naught else but a blue satin cape, smiled and tossed flower petals to the crowd. Then he smiled at J. P. And the disdainful patrician, seized by a sudden and unforeseen love for the circus, beamed back.

At this precise moment, the twenty-seventh elephant decided to relieve her self, and thus a sizeable mound plopped upon the pavement. J.P., still beaming and certainly not looking down, placed a pump squarely in the middle of this ball of elephant dung, found him self flipping up and then back down, to hit his head upon the tarmac and thus black out, quite oblivious to the approach of a team of eight rather hefty horses drawing the steam calliope that always ended any circus parade.

Ah, but as the crowd screamed, the spangled Ganymede saw J. P's plight. With consummate grace he leapt down from his howdah, and snatched up the recumbent unconscious just before an on-rushing Percheron might have squashed him. The crowd cheered, and Junius Pieter Morton opened his eyes to find himself in the arms of a gorgeous dream.

"You are hurt, Signore?"

"No, no, I...I think not."

"Still, you have hit your head."

The young man set J. P. down on his feet.

"But I seem..." J.P. felt the back of his head. There was a tender spot but no blood. "...seem to be uninjured."

"Still, Signore, someone must escort you to home. Is it far? Perhaps a hansom cab?"

"No, no, thank you. We're here, in fact, that very door," said J.P., pointing to the little entrance just around the corner from the tower's hulking base.

"Here? But Signore..."

"I have an apartment in the tower."

"Ah, then I shall accompany you myself," said the performer while he looked up in awe.

"You are too kind," beamed an equally awed J. P. as he fumbled for the key, and the loud wheezing of the calliope made further conversation impossible.

Strange how the gilded cage of the elevator suddenly reminded one of a circus menagerie. Then the arrow on the dial hit seven and the wire gates were slid aside. Stanny had certainly created a fine little foyer.

"Is like a little palazzo in my country," said the young man.

"Yes, I suppose it is. A very little one, though. I have but five rooms here."

J.P's key turned in the lock. "Am I correct that your country is Italy?"

"Si, Signore. I am Guido Gambini, aerialist extraordinaire! At least that is what all of the posters say. And you are?"

They had entered a lovely Quatrocento antechamber with a large window overlooking the rooftop pleasure gardens.

"Junius."

"Ah, like the famous Caesar, and from this window you survey your empire?"

"Not quite, I merely rent this place. For entertaining and such. And it's Junius Pieter Morton, not Julius. But to my friends I am just J.P."

"Well, Signore J. P., I think we should put you into the bed. No? Which way?"

Now J. P. rather liked that thought. He led the way to the salon, quite forgetting the presence of the red velvet swing.

"Fantástico!" Said Guido, when he saw the swing, "You were possibly expecting me?"

"Well, no...the previous tenant...ah, but...yes, isn't it perfect?"

And it was, for Guido threw aside his cape with a grand flourish (Oh how J. P. beamed to see that finely carved and naked chest.), and reached up (Those sinewy arms.), and hoisted (Oh, the biceps!) himself to stand (Such thighs!) upon the swing.

"Those hooks," said Guido, looking up to the ceiling, "they are strong?"

"I would hope, though I've never tested...yet I am told that the previous owner had many...guests swing upon..."

But Guido cut him off with a whoop as he swung higher and higher. J. P. staggered back to a sofa, loving the sight. So much closer than a box seat, even one by the center ring. Guido seized the ropes and turned himself upside down and did a headstand on the wildly swinging red velvet seat, arms straight out, legs splayed, thighs oh so very taut....like an upended version of Leonardo's drawing of the Vitruvian man. Then the aerialist extraordinaire reversed himself again and leapt off the still lunging trapeze to land and bow directly in front of his host.

"Bravo! Bravisimo Guido!" Shouted a wildly applauding J. P.

"Ah, I think that you are well indeed, Signore. But I also think you must rest for a while, and then...I will have two tickets waiting for you for tonight's performance. How do you think of that, Mr. Junius Morton?

"I think very well of that, Signore Gambini, but I shall only want one ticket. And that only if you and your guest will join me here afterwards for dinner."

"Then you will have but one ticket, Signore J. P., and in turn, I will be the only one to have dinner with you."

Had not a subtle signal been gloriously transferred? Guido gathered up his cape, bowed with a grand "Arrivederchi," and made his exit. J.P. did a little dance for joy and then, because the apartment had no kitchen, used the newly installed telephone to ring up Delmonico's for the later delivery of a romantic dinner. And, ah yes, maid-service— Stanny's mirrored bed could certainly do with an airing.

For J.P., that evening's edition of The Greatest Show on Earth had seemed as "Ho Hum" as any night at the Metropolitan Opera—<u>Aida</u>, but with twenty-eight elephants!—until that thrilling moment in the second half when the ring master's voice boomed out the words: "...wonderman of flight, master of terpsichorean trajectories, triumphant titan of trapeziasts, airborn Apollo of the center ring....Ladies, Gentlemen and Children of All Ages...the great Guido Gambini!" And there he was, Apollo striding to the center of the center ring.

Four carbon-arc spots followed him as he flung away his cape and reached for the white cotton rope, then hand over hand—and only hands— effortlessly pulled himself up and up and up, sixty feet, to the silver bar of his trapeze. J. P. was thoroughly transfixed.

Guido stood upon his bar, and with a sweeping gesture such as may only be mustered by circus folk and premier danseurs of the ballet, bowed to his audience, and then winked to the lone occupant of box number twenty-two. Guido twirled within the ropes and stood on his head and winked again. He balanced one-handed on a chair and waved with the other. J.P sheepishly waved back. Guido finished his act by falling forward (Such a gasp!), and catching himself with his heels (A greater gasp!), and after waving to resounding cheers, he blew a kiss to box twenty two. J.P. threw decorum to the wind and blew one back. Then his hero reached out for a line, and twisting again, hand over hand, descended unto the sawdust. The wide-armed walk around the ring, the wild cheers, the winsome bows, the wanton winks, and then once more wrapped in his blue silk cape, Guido whirled away to his dressing room. J.P. did not wait for the grand parade finale. He raced upstairs to his Zanadu in order to light candles, fluff pillows, and decide upon the proper arrangements of Delmonico delicacies.

Now, now—do not expect some cloud to obscure the moon, or a jealous villain to intrude, or even the ghost of Stanford White to ruin this evening. And no—those of you who feel terribly clever—the ceiling hooks will not give way. We're dealing with perfection here. Perhaps not the wan literary perfection of a short story by O'Henry, or even the dark perfection of an Edgar Allen Poe, but only the completely happy and libidinous perfection of J. P's life.

He answered the door chime. There stood a most dapper Guido: snappy two-tone shoes, tan trousers, seersucker jacket, bow tie, straw boater floating above jet black curls, coal black shining eyes, insouciant smile, and a lovely bouquet of roses. Do you see what I mean? Perfect.

So was the dinner. As the white wine warmed them, their jackets were removed. Oysters Rockefeller encouraged the first overtures. Both discovered that they were not only unencumbered by any relationships, but orphans as well. Bowties were undone. Guido thought the ensuing soupe de poissons to be "almost as good as suppe de pesce di Napoli." Aha, Guido was a Neopolitan. "Ah yes, Vesuvius reflected in the bay." The last of the white was drained. "Was not Italy the loveliest place on Earth?" The Bordeaux poured. "Was not New York the most exciting? And I would love to show you the sights." Now waistcoats were shed. During the entré—Delmonico Steaks of course—Guido asked about the curious presence of that red velvet swing in the "salone."

"This apartment was the creation of a famous architect, who died two weeks ago, shot by a jealous husband. Sad story, Guido, for the murderer's wife had, before their marriage, dallied here in these very rooms. The swing, you see, was added to the décor to serve as a tool of seduction."

"Oh la la, Signor J.P. I can see many possibilities."

"Indeed. It is said that many young ladies had swung upon it for the architect's pleasure. And sometimes in the nude. Ah, but now we have dessert...and champagne."

Peche Melba. Dom Pérignon, Grand Cru. Stiff starched collars were discarded with the robust popping of a cork.

"A toast, Guido. To the red velvet swing!"

"Si, Signore J. P. A la trappizzio di velluto rosso!"

"It sounds so much better in Italian."

"Si. Everything does. But now, think of seeing the possibilities of this swing being performed on by an Italian."

Needless to say the dining room was abandoned as had been the jackets, bowties waistcoats and collars. But the champagne was allowed to accompany them into the salon.

"Oh, but Signore, I seem to have forgotten to bring my costume." Guido smiled as he sat back upon the swing.

"Really? What ever shall we do?" said J.P. facing him from the opposite love seat and playing the Cheshire Cat.

"Ah, but we Italians are very resourceful, for God has given some of us an even better costume."

And now began a sinuous shedding. J.P. had never been to see the likes of Little Egypt performing her 'strip tease,' but he could not imagine it to have been as delectable as this. Oh, to have had a small orchestra hidden in the next room. Ah, well.

Guido kicked away his shoes and slipped off his stockings, then stood upon the gently swaying swing to balance with grace and thus unbutton his shirt. It too was discarded, and J.P. beamed at the sight of that splendid torso. Then the trapezziast undid his belt, and reclined upon the swing.

"Now you must assist, Signor J.P."

He swung further, pointing his legs forward.

"The pants, J.P., take them."

J.P. reached forward to seize the cuffs and thus pull the trousers off on the back swing. And he gasped, for Guido wore no undergarment. There he was, fully nude, laughing, furiously swinging higher and higher, legs spread wide, arms strong on the ropes, back arched, and as he swung his male member grew fully rampant. And J.P. thought, "Oh thank you, God, and Naples, and Stanny, and Barnum and Bailey—and Father's coupons!"

Guido proceeded to go through as much of his act as was possible on such a low swing. J.P even ran off to the dining room to fetch him a small side chair for the balancing bit. Of course everything was...well...so different... without the spangled tights, but with...oh how might a decadent ring master have said it? The amazing apendage? That male flagpole of desire? Ah yes, "A prodigious perpendicular, so pregnantly patriotic in its priapic portrait of puerile perfection!"

Alas, one part of the act was impossible: the final heel-catching bit. So Guido simply used a forward swing to leap for a spectacular dismount, landing upon the loveseat, his knees astride J.P's legs, his groin grinding into J.P's chest., his torso towering above that adoring face. Then he bent down for a long and oh-so-lovely kiss.

"Now J.P., We will become a 'duo-act' and you must change into your 'costume' and join me in the center ring."

How remarkable it was to have, not a cool valet, but a fevered Italian undress one! J..P. emerged from his cocoon of fashionable propriety to see himself most circusorially spangled with luminous droplets of the sweat of desire.

"We must begin our new act with you on the swing, J.P. Come. Sit."

J.P. sat. Guido stood behind. Those bronzed arms reached out and around and tugged the ropes to swing the patrician into arcs of ecstasy.

"Very good, Signore, now arch your back. More. Ah, that is right J.P. Curve. Yes! Now you are one with the trapeze. And now I will really swing you."

Oh he did that! Guido gave J.P. a greater push every time that he swung. Soon his toes were able to touch the ceiling, but more wonderful, with every backward pass his lips were able to graze Guido's gorgeous genitalia. And J.P's flagpole was rising to its own pirapic salute of cross-cultural cheer.

"Now, J. P., now I join you on the swing!"

Guido leapt to grab the red velvet ropes. He held his body rigid, horizontal, hovering directly over J.P. Guido lowered him self with those iron arms to lie upon J.P. with a flying kiss, and let centrifugal force press their bodies tighter. Then he raised himself again, swung his legs forward, and impaled his derrière on J.P's rigid penis. His arms pulled up and gravity pulled down and centrifugal gyrations gave...ah, not even the most decadent of ring masters could have imagined an alliteration that might do justice to the sensations that J.P. experienced. Thank goodness that the walls were thick, for their cries of rapture surely would have rivaled a calliope in volume.

This time the dismount was one of, well, intricate entanglement. Guido taught J.P the graces of the circus bow, all the while laughing at how grace was somewhat defeated by dual erections. Then they retired to tug on, among other things, the many toggle switches of Stanny's mirrored bed. Perhaps his ghost smiled.

At breakfast, courtesy of Delmonico's of course, Guido told J.P. of several other circus performers who shared their "proclivities." The word sounded so charming when delivered with a Neapolitan accent. And such a list: Heinrich, the bare back rider; Jean-Claude, the contortionist; Alonzo, of high wire fame; and the most fascinating of all—Felix the sword swallower—and fire-eater!

"How remarkable!" said J.P., "Do you think that they would enjoy being entertained?"

"Si, J.P. We could present a very special circus."

"With, perhaps, a very small and select audience?"

"Per que no?"

And thus was born The Gayest Show On Earth.

Two weeks later, the last night of Barnum and Bailey's run, all was in readiness. Burton and Jenkins looked quite dashing in their hussars' uniforms. The butler stood at the door, and the valet manned the bar. Ev and Bev, charmingly attired in bare-back rider tutus, tittered with silver trays of delicacies from—where else but Delmonico's? And J.P. strutted about in the high silk hat and red tails of a ring master. Guido and his cast 'dressed' and tried toggles in the bedroom.

Then the bell rang. Gus St. Gaudins was accompanied by John Singer Sergeant, and a very tall fellow from Philadelphia named Eakins. Another ring announced James Hazen Hyde, and a friend named Chauncy. Hyde looked at the décor and pronounced it to be "Just too too Duveen." There were only a few more guests, to make twelve in all, for such events must be kept very private.

I shall not regale you with all of the performing wonders that ensued, except to report the one minor disaster of the evening. It seems that Felix got somewhat carried away, slightly singeing Sergeant in the nether regions. Ah, but béarnaise sauce does wonders as a treatment for overheated meat. John was quite amused, and Bev loved playing nurse. Otherwise the evening was such a success that for the next twelve years whenever Barnum and Bailey played The Madison Square Garden, The Gayest Show On Earth was performed in the tower.

And J.P. pronounced it all to be "Quite Perfect."

A Marvellous Party

"Everyone's here and frightfully gay.'
Nobody cares what people say,
Though the Riviera
Seems really much queerer
Than Rome at its height,
Yesterday night – "

Noel Coward: *I've Been To A Marvellous Party,* 1939.

Having little else to do, the Villa Frivola smiles upon the tiny port of St. Jean-Cap Ferrat. This is not unusual for, like every other *maison de plaisance* on the Riviera, the villa resembles the neo-classical fantasy of a preternaturally happy cake decorator. But yesterday night La Frivola's smile was even warmer, as its eaves had been strung with colored lights, the garden illuminated by flocks of paper lanterns, and every window glimmered from the dancing refractions of candle light and crystal chandeliers.

The port had the good manners to smile back. This being the high season, not one slip remained un-shipped, or must one say un-boated? An entire fleet of pleasure craft bobbed at anchor: yawls, ketches, schooners, motor cruisers, even four steam yachts—no, make that three—the Duke of Bermoldesy's boasted two stacks. He had jokingly named it H.M.S. Behemoth. And every one of these carnivalesque caravels was bedazzled with myriad lights that twinkled in gently swaying loops strung from mast to mast, or in the Duke's case, from stack to stack. Smaller lanterns flitted like nautical fireflies from yacht to yacht to shore. They hung from the sternposts of launches ferrying guests to the villa.

Nannette de Finchon, toast of both Belgravia and Mayfair, had rented La Frivola in order to give another of her annual *Belle Nuits de Beaux Arts*. The theme this season was to be "Creatures of the Sea," thus the launches looked rather like the return of the fishing fleet, albeit with a decidedly outsized catch. Giant gold lamé lobsters, one of them the duke, waved to bugle-beaded starfish. Taffeta anemones slithered up the gangway accompanied by sequined sea horses. A mauve sea serpent wandered somewhat blindly across the Place de la Port. Whole schools of iridescent fish floundered through the streets, and a trio of purple porpoises waddled up the steps to the villa's entrance.

In the salon, two dapper men in their mid-thirties chose not to be aquatic. Ivor Novello and Noel Coward wore summer tails. Nannette had pooh-poohed them, but Ivor replied that the piano could not possibly be played by either giant lobster claws or fish fins, and since, as Noel had so famously stated, their presence depended upon "a talent to amuse", the hostess forgave them, adding: "But as penance you shall also have to be the judges for the best costume."

"Friendships dashed," sighed Noel.

"Girls bellowing, boys sobbing," added Ivor.

"And the horrid prospect of bribes," purred Noel.

"Done!" beamed both.

"Ah, Nannette's naughty boys," said the statuesque hostess, "and worth every smirk." She swept off to the dining room to inspect mountains of *fruits de mer*. By the way, she had to sweep a good bit, for as "Neptunia," her train of spangled seaweed and fishnet trailed for a dozen feet or so. Her equally spangled trident had a tendency to nip the chandeliers. Nannette had cajoled Cecil Beaton into designing this unwieldy maritime ensemble. Noel and Ivor stayed behind in the salon and languished as elegant bookends for the grand piano.

Else wise, Nannette had gotten Cecil to decorate the villa with several more miles of blue and green spangled fishnet. It dripped from chandeliers, swagged off to cornices, and then swooped down to entrap the mirrors and ensnare a reef's worth of pink <u>papier-maché</u> sea shells. *Tres Nautique*! Netting had also ensnarled the piano, but upon arrival, Ivor had torn it away, and Dear Cecil, in a fit of most unpacific pique, stormed off to his digs in order to change into his costume.

Then the first guests announced themselves by pulling on the tasseled cord attached to a rhinestone encrusted ship's bell that Cecil had installed in the foyer. Thus encased, it rang with rather a clunk.

"Do you hear chimes, Noel?" asked Ivor.

"More likely a knell."

Nannette heard it too. She plucked up her trident, pulled in her nets and trawled through to the foyer. "Ah, Nada and Nounou and Nell, how good of you to come," exclaimed the distant hostess.

"How prescient of you, Noel." said Ivor, "Shall you or I be the first to tickle the ivories?"

"You tickle. Quentin says you do that rather well."

"Ivories, not toes."

"Nonetheless, you do the tickling, while I find the W.C and tinkle."

"A watery descant, how appropriate."

Ivor flipped his tails and assumed the piano bench. He played "By the Sea" to the un-rhythmic accompaniment of the ship's bell's clunks, as more sea life funneled into the foyer.

The porpoises, Nounou, Nada and Nell, swam into view. They were followed by the four-humped sea-serpent, which had rather a bad time as it tried to snake its way through to the salon. It was soon noised about that in the serpent's head was Nancy Mitford. Her beautiful sisters were the humps. Upon returning, Noel remarked not very sotto voce to Ivor that this might be the first time that the celebrated sisters had co-operated on anything. He should have realized that most of the serpent's un-seaworthy undulations were the result of bickering beneath the folds.

Soon the salon was crowded with ersatz sea life, much of it becoming entangled in Cecil's nets. One lobster had a terrible time trying to claw its martini glass, and both sea horses begged the waiters for much longer straws. The octopus was lucky, for two of its arms incongruously, yet quite happily, ended in hands. But every time that the starfish turned, one of its wired arms knocked another creature's drink away. It was obvious that these costumes would not last long. Soon there must be a deluge of doffing.

"I think, Dear Noel," said Ivor at the end of a particularly enervating arpeggio, "that your turn to tickle has arrived. Besides, all of this delirious diluvia has driven me to drink." Noel obligingly flipped his tails. He launched into a strangely jazzy version of "Britannia Rules the Waves". Unfortunately, since jazz and patriotism seldom mix, it rather sank. That was when the bell clunked again, and then the sound of a flute and tambourines filtered in from the foyer.

This new music silenced not only the piano, but the crowd as well. All eyes, as well as fins, claws and tentacles, were directed towards the entry. And there appeared, playing the flute, the Aladdin of a Christmas pantomime. Jaunty red fez, small sequin-embroidered vest, gossamer pantaloons, slippers with upturned points...perfectly traditional, but with one stunning difference. The Aladdin of the 'pantos' is a britches role, meaning a male played by a fetching female. This Aladdin was a fetching young man of divine proportions. Noel was transfixed, as were the lobster ducale, a seahorse and the octopus. Ivor was hardly oblivious.

Alas, Aladdin stepped aside. Two rather beefy yet similarly dressed young men struck their tambourines, and then rolled in a huge pink scallop shell. Both Noel and Ivor laughed for they knew who would play its pearl. Aladdin resumed his flute as the two Aladdettes pried open the shell, and there arose, swirling in a pearlescent silk robe, Dear Cecil.

Well, there was nothing for it but to give a huge round of applause. A beaming albeit very baroque pearl was surrounded by swarms of happy cheering fish, although it must be noted that a certain atristo-crustacean, as well as the many-armed mollusk, had slithered to the side of the flute player. The equally enraptured seahorse, alas, became entrapped in some netting. And Noel, once the cheers had died away, found himself not very surreptitiously ogling the young man while quietly playing "Mad About The Boy."

The boy in question duly noticed. He smiled back, quite invidious to inviting fins, claws and tentacles. Noel beamed and reprised the song with ebonized fervor. Then, as though borne upon an unseen magic carpet, Aladdin floated to the piano. Noel was delighted to discover that his music might have such levitating properties.

"Vous et Monsieur Coward, non?" said a pleasant voice in Moroccan flavored French.

"I am suddenly pleased to admit it."

"I like very much your music."

"And I've been admiring your...flute. But who are you?"

"I am al Hadin."

"Not the costume, Dear Boy, you."

"Not Aladdin. That is one of your ungainly English corruptions. My name, Monsieur Coward, is Armand al Hadin."

"Please, call me Noel."

"My thanks Monsieur Noel, did you enjoy our entrance?"

"Hm, how shall I...ah yes...

> Dear Cecil arrived in a sea shell,
> Made of sisal and sequins and glue.
> He's my favorite designer,
> But it would have been finer,
> If that seashell's pearl had been you."

"I am flattered, Monsieur. Limericks are so very English. Do you find it easy to make them?"

"Only when I am inspired."

"Ah, then you must hear Arab poetry."

"I'm seeing it."

Armand laughed. Then Noel was nudged by Ivor. "I say, Old Boy, you seem to have lost interest in playing...the piano."

And indeed, for Noel, the piano, the party, everything but Armand had, as though at the cinema, gone into soft focus. Ivor graciously assumed the keyboard, while Aladdin and his new genie escaped to the garden, and thereafter disappeared into the star lit night. It was Ivor alone who gave the prize...well of course...to Cecil.

The next morning Armand awoke in Noel's rented flat to hear piano music coming from the other room, and then heard his host's voice warbling the following...

> Aladdin

> A lady I know,
> Always stops at her door.
> Her kissless "Good Night"
> Means "Sorry, no more."

Each beau slinks away,
Cursing the night,
Quite sad that she won't let a lad in.

Well I've met a lad,
Of Arabian air,
With dark glowing eyes,
And smooth savoir-faire,
When we got to my door,
I opened it wide.
Can't help it if I let that lad in.

We flew up the stairs that led to my flat.
The fire had died to soft coals.
We stoked them and then, doffing fez and top hat,
We stoked them all over again.

A lad and a lad,
With fires aglow,
Recline on the carpet
As the world flies below.
They slowly entwine,
Like the carpet's design,
So glad that a lad let a lad in.

We both made a wish for a genie to grant,
But there wasn't a brass lamp in sight,
So we stroked something else, though it wasn't a lamp,
And what issued was damp and milk white.

Sweet Arab dreams,
And desert desire.
Fly off on the carpet;
Aladdins on fire.
Genies will grant
All wishes of love,
Whenever a lad lets a lad in.

Once a music rack has been folded away, it is amazing what acrobatic ballets might be achieved on the top of a grand piano, especially if the host is able to keep one hand free and thereby provide a musical accompaniment. Thus more than ebonies or ivories were lovingly tickled on a sun lit Sunday morning. And of course the Villa Frivola continued to smile.

The Garden of Earthly Delights

Such a lovely day, such happy sun light, and such a very pretty place. The brand new eight-millimeter color movie camera pans first along the high stone wall ringing the garden. Banks of lovingly tended flowers are punctuated by reproductions of famous statues. On one side a bust of Hermes, after Praxiteles, surmounts a truncated ionic column. And further down, Michelangelo's David surveys the scene. At the rear hollyhocks have been artfully overgrown to make an innocent frame for Zeus Caressing Ganymede. And on the other side, busts of Hadrian and Antinous gaze at each other from atop their own ionic aeries, so tastefully separated by a bed of variegated pansies.

Then the lens pulls back to reveal a perfectly manicured lawn framing the classical coping of the swimming pool. Four urns topped with rose bush crowns guard its corners. A long line of lapis lazuli tiles is reflected in the dancing azure water. Dancing firstly, because the rose bedecked bronze reproduction of Brussels's Manikin Piss unleashes his thin stream into the pool, but mostly because Greg is swimming.

The camera follows as he takes long, sure strokes, lapping past the lapis. A trim man in his forties, well-tanned, and wearing tasteful black trunks. At the far end he flips for his turn and spots the camera. Big smile as he swims up to the edge of the pool. The camera operator's hand comes into view, displaying a bracelet that sparkles in the sun. The hand presents a cocktail to Greg, garnished with a little pink paper umbrella. Greg takes it, blows a kiss to the camera, and raises a toast. Camera out.

A new sequence: one which Greg is obviously shooting from the edge of the pool. The house matches the gardens. Colonial? But of course, with red brick facade, nice green window shutters, rose-covered trellises between the windows on either side of the screened porch, and two more statues. To the left an Apollo Belvedere raises his languid arm, and on the right, the Discus Thrower prepares to let fly.

Now the camera zooms in to the porch. There's a flash of color beyond the screens. Then the door opens and Edgrina comes out with a tray of drinks and canapés. The dress is very summery, a pattern of pink and yellow hydrangeas. And so much more tasteful than those awful things that Bess Truman wears. A simple string of cultured pearls and the rhinestone bracelet complete the ensemble. Edgrina is well past fifty and a bit on the pudgy side.

The hostess gestures toward a little green wicker table and two cast-iron garden chairs. Greg's hand flips into camera view, splashing water, and Edgrina retreats while flashing her finger in a "No, no, no" signal. Any reader of lips could have made out the words: "Oh you naughty boy!" Then Edgrina sits, patting the other chair seat, winking and giving a "come hither" look.

The camera sidles along the coping edge, still centered on Edgrina. Then it lurches upward. Greg is obviously leaving the pool. Edgrina grows to fill the screen as Greg takes the camera closer. Waist up view now, and we see freckles on the somewhat flabby arms. Closer still, and one might almost smell a cloying perfume. Head shot: dark flashing eyes, much mascara, and very rouged cheeks. Extreme close up: two fiery red lips constrict to a pout, purse to a kiss, and relax into a wide smile. Then a tongue rides lasciviously along the teeth. Camera out.

Now we will have to take up our own and very secret camera. Pan back as Greg lowers his trunks, and Edgrina sinks to her knees. Then, for modesty's sake, we quickly retreat through the screened porch, with all of its potted perennials, and further back through the dining room, done Duncan

Phyfe, of course. Pan right, for the bedroom door is open. Obviously Edgrina had to make some choices. Several flowered frocks are splayed upon the bed. And through an open closet door we can see a whole rack of dresses on one side, and men's suits on the other.

Our camera continues to the living room, quite masculine with a leather covered sofa and arm chairs. A large Georgian fireplace is surrounded by many framed photographs of famous politicos...and all effusively autographed. Pull back further, right out through the front door, then on down the front walk. Everything is more conservative out here. Each house is brick colonial indeed, all with reassuring rows of most regular windows. White classical moldings sing of the East coast. Virginia perhaps? Ah, but we'll know soon enough, for the last thing that our camera catches is the mailbox: It's an Arlington address. And under the owner's name are the words:

"Director, Federal Bureau of Investigation."

About the Author

Kenneth Craigside has spent a lifetime in the service of the theatre as a designer of lighting and scenery. Recently retired, he lives in Florida with his partner of eighteen years. Both are now in the service of a cat named Skitz. But said cat is not allowed in the library which holds a considerable collection devoted to history, art, and architecture. Mr. Craigside's method of writing is to search out history's cracks and plaster them over with exciting plausibilities. In the case of these stories the plaster has been stirred with liberal amounts of sensual fun.

www.ingramcontent.com/pod-product-compliance
Lightning Source LLC
Chambersburg PA
CBHW052041090426
42739CB00010B/2003